THE
LMS PACIFICS

J. W. P. ROWLEDGE
C.Eng, MI Mech E

DAVID & CHARLES
Newton Abbot   London
North Pomfret (Vt)

David & Charles books on locomotive classes

AC Electric Locomotives of British Rail, Brian
  Webb and John Duncan
The British Railcar – AEC to HST, R. M. Tufnell
The Deltic Locomotives of British Rail, Brian
  Webb
The Drummond Greyhounds of the LSWR,
  D. L. Bradley
Gresley Pacifics, O. S. Nock
GWR Stars Castles & Kings, O. S. Nock
Prototype Locomotives, R. M. Tufnell
Royal Scots & Patriots of the LMS, O. S. Nock
Southern King Arthur Family, O. S. Nock
Standard Gauge Great Western 4–4–0s,
  O. S. Nock
Standard Steam Locomotives of British Railways,
  R. P. Bradley
Stanier 4–6–0s of the LMS, Brian Reed and
  J. W. P. Rowledge
Sulzer Diesel Locomotives of British Rail, Brian
  Webb
*DC Electric Locomotives and Trains in the British
  Isles*, R. L. Vickers

British Library Cataloguing in Publication Data

Rowledge, J. W. P.
  The LMS Pacifics.—(David & Charles
  locomotive monographs)
  1. London, Midland and Scottish Railway—
  History 2. Locomotives—Great Britain—
  History—20th century
  I. Title
  385'.361'0941   TJ603.4.G72L65

  ISBN 0–7153–8776–6

© J. W. P. Rowledge 1987
First published 1987
Second impression 1987

Photoset by Northern Phototypesetting Company, Bolton
and printed in Great Britain
by Redwood Burn Limited, Trowbridge, Wilts
for David & Charles Publishers plc
Brunel House, Newton Abbot, Devon

Published in the United States of America
by David & Charles Inc
North Pomfret, Vermont 05053, USA

Acknowledgements

The pleasure in putting together this volume on
the Stanier Pacifics has been twofold, the first
recollections of an Engineering Apprenticeship at
Crewe Works 30 and more years ago when I
worked on several of the Pacifics or saw them
receiving attention or in traffic, the second the
professional relationship with working colleagues
who so generously passed over information to
augment my own researches. In particular
considerable help has been given by Brian
Radford, Ray Ellis, John Edgington and John
Boulton, the latter generously giving me all of his
notes put together as a Pupil in Crewe Works.
Others who have given help include Mr A. F.
Cook and Mr G. Wilson.

The following sources have been invaluable in
the research undertaken and the author is very
grateful to the staff of them for their help in
producing documents and allowing material to be
used:
  Public Records Office, Kew (and formerly the
  British Transport Historical Records)
  Public Relations Office, British Railways
  (London Midland Region), formerly at Euston
  National Railway Museum, York
  Institution of Mechanical Engineers
  The Railway Gazette.
In addition the author has made considerable use
of the library of The Railway Club, London.

Apart from the above, files of the following
magazines have been consulted:
  The Railway Magazine
  The Railway Observer (Railway Corres-
  pondence & Travel Society),
  Journal of the Stephenson Locomotive Society
  Railway World
  The Locomotive Magazine.
Many other published works have been
consulted, they being too numerous to mention
individually.

CONTENTS

CHAPTER ONE

GENESIS AND DEVELOPMENT OF THE STANIER PACIFICS

A decade after the Grouping of Britain's railways into the 'Big Four' the London Midland & Scottish Railway was still without a high-speed passenger locomotive capable of working day in and day out over the full length of its premier route between London and Glasgow. 'High Speed' is a relative term and in the 1930s referred to journeys completed at an average of 55–60mph with occasional bursts of around 70mph or so. The 'West Coast' route of the LMS connecting the English and Scottish cities was divided into two distinct geographical stages (it still is, but our modern-day electric locomotives are little affected by this factor), the southern end of some 240 miles between London and just to the north of Carnforth in Lancashire being relatively easy and the northern section of the remaining 160-odd miles consisting of two major 'humps' with summits in excess of 900ft and 1,000ft, dropping to sea level between them at the border city of Carlisle. In contrast the 'East Coast' route of the rival London & North Eastern Railway between London and the Scottish capital Edinburgh is relatively level, having much lower summits, but was already served by a growing fleet of Pacific locomotives capable of making a non-stop run of 392 miles, the distance from London to Edinburgh being slightly less than that to Glasgow. Prior to the Grouping there was no railway commercial incentive to provide either fast or non-stop services to Scotland, nor were there locomotives capable of undertaking such duties, apart from the fact that ownership was divided between two companies on the west side and three on the east. Overall times of Anglo-Scottish services were subject to a long-standing agreement dating back to the 'Races to the North' of 1888/1896 so that trains did not cover the journey in less than 8¼ hours! This agreement was terminated in 1932 and opened up a new era in Anglo-Scottish express services, but the LMS was in no position to take immediate advantage. The company still had not been able to introduce a new class of locomotive comparable with the Gresley Pacifics as immortalised by *Flying*

Scotsman; these locomotives had an easy time with the 8¼ hours timing and had been developed and improved so that tightened schedules were no problem. The working of The Flying Scotsman had captured public imagination, particularly with its non-stop summer schedule made possible by the use of a through corridor and gangwayed tender, so that the two sets of enginemen required could change over half way. The LMS urgently needed to do something about its second-place image.

At the Grouping there were but three classes of Pacific in Great Britain. The Great Western Railway had *The Great Bear* of 1908, the earliest British Pacific, which was a single example and so confined in its use that it really has no significant place in the history of British express services; in any case it was about to be rebuilt as a Castle Class 4–6–0. The next class was introduced by the Great Northern Railway which, as the southern partner in the East Coast route, passed to the LNER two Pacifics (and ten that were well on the way to completion). They were followed by another forty in 1924–5 as the Pacific type became the dominant express motive power on that side of Britain, eventually reaching 207 in number by the time that construction of LNER designs ceased. The other class comprised the five Raven Pacifics of the North Eastern Railway built in 1922–4, which never equalled the Gresley engines and passed into oblivion in 1936–7. The LMS never matched the number of LNER Pacifics, as much due to operating practice as the long delay in meeting the demand for such a locomotive.

The first West Coast Pacific did not materialise until 1933, but 20 years earlier the Caledonian Railway, the northern partner on the route, considered the use of a Pacific type and progressed matters to the extent of producing weight diagrams. Four were contemplated, to be shared amongst Kingmoor (Carlisle), Polmadie (Glasgow) and Perth (2, 1 and 1 respectively) but evidently J. F. McIntosh, the Locomotive Superintendent of the 'Caley' did not seek

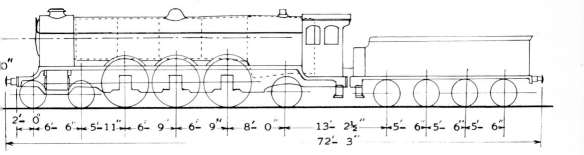

approval for their construction. The drawing shows their outline and principal dimensions; noticeable is the great length which suggests that the estimated weight of 90 tons would have been handsomely exceeded, especially when the usually massive construction of the company's locomotives is taken into account. The grate area was half as much again as that of the McIntosh 4–6–0 classes, but it would have restricted the Pacific to about 1,300dbhp (with a maximum of 1,850), assuming good steaming, which was doubtful with tubes 22ft long. In all probability the appearance that year of the London & North Western Railway's 4–6–0 Claughton Class prompted the choice of four cylinders. The justification for a Pacific was almost certainly the cost of providing and manning double-headed trains between Carlisle and Glasgow. McIntosh was constantly challenged by his directors over coal consumption, but by the autumn of 1913 he was looking forward to retirement. It fell to his successor, William Pickersgill, to provide the final Caledonian express locomotives, and he chose to stay with 4–6–0 designs.

On the West Coast route matters stayed much as before when after the end of World War I the LNWR continued to build its four-cylinder Claughton 4–6–0s in substantial numbers. The CR continued to rely on its fleet of McIntosh inside cylinder 4–6–0 and 4–4–0 classes, the Pickersgill 4–6–0s being too few in number and far below expectations to have any significance. Then in the final year before the Grouping took full effect a new influence came in the shape of George Hughes who, as Chief Mechanical Engineer of the combined LNWR and Lancashire & Yorkshire Railway, chose to draft his own design of four-cylinder 4–6–0 onto West Coast workings. A batch of 25 was ordered in 1922 and put to work between Crewe and Carlisle in 1922–3, augmented by a further 20 in 1924–5,

Fig 1 Proposed Caledonian Railway 4–6–2, 1913. Both narrow and wide firebox schemes were prepared in October 1913 by J. F. Macintosh, CME of the Caledonian Railway. The narrow firebox proposal had a slightly longer coupled wheelbase of 14ft 4in (equally divided). Other dimensions were:

	Narrow firebox	Wide firebox
Cylinders (4)	16inx26in	16inx26in
Bogie wheels	3ft 6in	3ft 6in
Coupled wheels	6ft 6in	6ft 6in
Trailing wheels	4ft 6in	4ft 6in
Boiler maximum diameter	5ft 8in	5ft 8in
Tube length	20ft 6in	22ft 0in
Heating surface		
– tubes	2,456sq ft	2,440 sq ft
– firebox	172sq ft	158sq ft
Superheater	516sq ft	516sq ft
Grate area	27sq ft	37sq ft
Boiler pressure	180lb/sq in	180lb/sq in
Locomotive weight (estimated)	90tons	90tons
Tractive effort	24,600lb	24,600lb

Based on information supplied by the National Railway Museum.

which were the remnants of a 1922 order for no fewer than 60 LYR Baltic tanks (4–6–4T), only ten of which emerged as designed, with the balance of 30 never built! Having acquired responsibility for West Coast motive power in 1922 Hughes had to await the formation of the LMS in 1923 before he could look seriously at enhanced designs for the Anglo-Scottish trains.

Despite uncertainties inevitable in the early days of any organisation there was a distinct possibility of a Pacific design appearing fairly soon on the rails of the new company. Had the system of management of the LMS been anything like that of the LNER or GWR such a locomotive could have been agreed upon and in service by about 1926–7, but because responsibility was divided between the operating side and the mechanical engineer it became impossible to agree even the basic features of the urgently needed locomotives. The divided form of management controlling motive power and running was inherited from the Midland Railway, and its perpetuation was ensured by the appointment of so many former MR men to top places. George Hughes became CME in preference to Sir Henry Fowler who had held that post on the MR until the Grouping; the latter became Hughes's deputy and so, perhaps without intent, ensured that Midland practice dominated all matters. The contrast in operating practice between the MR and LNWR is well enough known not to have to describe it in detail, but essentially the former provided frequent light trains and the latter less frequent but much heavier trains. The Midland Railway also placed considerable emphasis on keeping loads within the prescribed limits, adding assisting engines almost at the drop of a hat, while the latter let the enginemen get on with it. Hughes did not remain in the chair long enough to sort matters and impose his ideas, retiring in September 1925, to be followed by Fowler. Because running affairs were in the hands of J. E. Anderson, another Midland man, the influence of Derby became supreme. How the LMS was to pay for this (and even British Rail to the present day) is well known for the retardation of locomotive development on the railway that afflicted the first decade of its existence, when only non-Derby personages really provided first-rate designs.

By virtue of the appointment of Hughes as Chief Mechanical Engineer of the LMS, Horwich, situated on the northern fringe of the South Lancashire industrial belt and far less accessible than either Crewe or Derby, became the centre of mechanical affairs of the company. Had Hughes been willing to move to Crewe, events on the LMS (and later on BR) could well have taken a very different course, for he and his staff would have been more in contact with LMS management and been able to speak more frequently than they could from the isolation of mid-Lancashire! However, tentative proposals for a Pacific locomotive were formulated during 1923, but neither the operating nor motive power officers displayed any interest, for they had decided to impose the Midland policy of short frequent trains on the West Coast services; their interest lay in small locomotives and the Midland compound 4–4–0 design was adopted as the prime passenger type for new construction. Put into practice, the Midland style timetable was very quickly shown to be unacceptable on the West Coast services, as much to the public who did not appreciate the change as to those who were well experienced in handling that traffic. Despite an early reversion to the former system of timetabling, the building of locomotives suited only to the discredited policy continued. The Hughes 4–6–0s gave undistinguished service between Crewe and Carlisle, rarely visiting London, and the real mainstay between London and Carlisle continued to be the LNWR Claughton class, aided by other LNWR types at times. It became the practice to change engines at Carnforth, using LNWR engines to the south and LMS 4–4–0 compounds, in pairs, to the north on the heavier through trains – but the urgency for a more powerful type remained.

The direct cause for the preparation of a Pacific scheme in 1924 in greater detail was the unrelated problem of the East Midlands to London coal traffic on the former Midland Railway main line on which massive coal trains slowly made their way into the Home Counties over a far from easy road, almost inevitably double-headed, at a cost that was constantly under scrutiny. The need for a larger type of locomotive that could do the job single-handed was all too obvious, but any attempt to overcome the problem was inhibited by the maximum permitted axle loading enforced by the civil engineer. Hughes' solution was a 2–8–2 locomotive, and with his 'workshops hat' on he immediately proposed a corresponding design of 4–6–2 having as much in common as possible with the eight-coupled goods. By June 1924 the Pacific proposal was ready for submission to the operating and locomotive committees of the LMS. Interesting points to note were the retention of four cylinders, and with the realisation that there was a need for a greater coal capacity, the eight-wheeled tender was shown to contain eight tons in contrast to the Derby standard tender which could take only 5½ tons. Water capacity was not seen as a problem as there were sufficient water troughs between London and Carlisle and in any case non-stop running was not intended. The proposed locomotive was to have two sets of valve gear for the four cylinders, based on the layout of Hughes' 4–6–0 class, but compounding was not considered as he had long before discarded that principal as irrelevant to express locomotives. The size of the cylinders was determined by his unshakeable conviction that boiler pressure

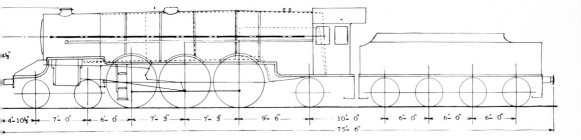

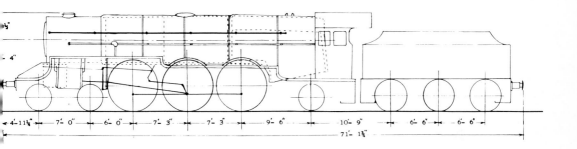

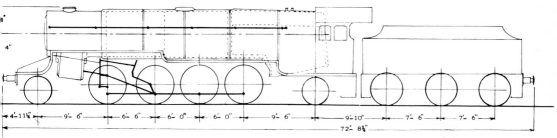

Fig 2 (*top*) Proposed Hughes 4–6–2, 1924.
Fig 3 (*right*) Proposed Fowler 4–6–2, 1925.
Fig 4 (*above*) Proposed Fowler 2–8–2, 1925.

Two of the 1924–1926 proposals for West Coast Pacific locomotives. The 2–8–2 goods locomotive is added to show the dominance of workshop thinking for standardisation and the fact that its proposed tender was adopted with little change for the first Stanier Pacifics. *Drawings prepared from information supplied by Mr J. B. Radford.*
The basic dimensions of the three types were:

Proposed design	Hughes 4–6–2	Fowler 4–6–2 Compound	Fowler 2–8–2 Compound
LOCOMOTIVE			
Cylinders (4)	18½inx26in	16¾inx26in(o) 23⅝inx26in (i)	16¾inx26in(o) 23⅝inx26in (i)
Bogie wheels	3ft 6½in	3ft 3in	–
Leading wheels	–	–	3ft 6½in
Coupled wheels	6ft 9in	6ft 9in	5ft 3in
Trailing wheels	3ft 9in	3ft 6½in	3ft 6½in
Boiler barrel (internal diam.)	5ft 9in	5ft 9⅞in	5ft 9⅞in
Tube length	19ft 0in	17ft 0in	17ft 0in

Proposed design	Hughes 4–6–2	Fowler 4–6–2 Compound	Fowler 2–8–2 Compound
Firebox casing length	*	8ft 0in	8ft 0in
Tubes – number/ diameter	168/2¼in	172/2in	172/2in
– number/ diameter	32/5¼in	32/5⅛in	32/5⅛in
Heating surface			
– tubes	2,715sq ft	2,357sq ft	2,357sq ft
– firebox	230sq ft	221sq ft	221sq ft
– Total	2,945sq ft	2,578sq ft	2,578sq ft
Superheater	600sq ft	631sq ft	631sq ft
Grate area	42sq ft	43.5sq ft	43.5sq ft
Boiler pressure	180lb/sq in	240lb/sq in	240lb/sq. in
Weight (estimated)	95 tons	91 tons	99 tons
Tractive effort	33,600lb	34,600lb	44,400lb
TENDER			
Wheels	3ft 9in	4ft 3in	4ft 3in
Coal	8 tons	5½ tons	8 tons
Water	5,000 gallons	3,500 gallons	4,000 gallons
Weight (estimated)	54tons 0cwt	42tons 14cwt	52tons 10cwt

*Not shown on drawing.

Fig 5 Composite diagram showing cylinder and bearing centres of Fowler compound Pacific. *By Permission of the Institution of Mechanical Engineers, Paper No 457, Journal 190.*

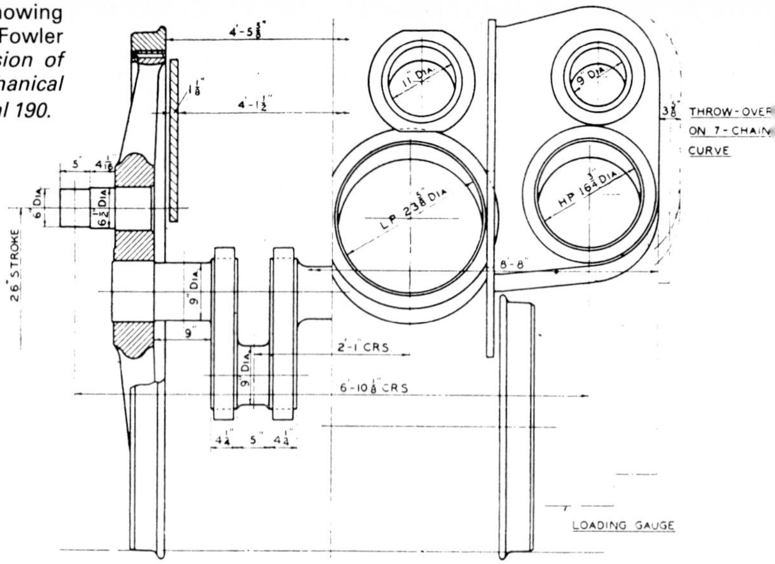

should not exceed 180 lb sq in. The 'Midland Faction' point of view was expressed by the motive power officers' belief that a three-cylinder version would do and he submitted a counter proposal at the end of the year. This double project was mentioned in locomotive committee minutes only in July 1924 when it was recorded that a new type of heavier freight locomotive was under consideration, which would be able to dispense with double-heading on the Toton to Brent coal trains, but it was added that bridges would need to be strengthened – the passenger version was not even mentioned.

As soon as Hughes retired Derby became the principal design centre, although neither Crewe nor Horwich ceased to put forward their own views. With Fowler in charge compound designs came to the fore, and after the consideration of a 4–6–0 type thoughts again turned to a Pacific. The provision of better motive power for the Midland Division coal trains was still an unresolved matter, and as before parallel schemes for a 4–6–2 and 2–8–2 standardised as much as possible were hatched at Derby. Perhaps thinking that he would acquire irrefutable proof of the superiority of compounding, and fully realising that he would gain a greater measure of support from Anderson and the motive power department, Fowler visited France in October 1925 where he contacted the major railways. Possibly much to his surprise, he found that there was no universal acceptance of compounding, although a fuel economy of 10 percent to 15 percent was claimed by some quarters, countered by an increase of up to eight percent in

maintenance costs. He also found that there were no strong views on boiler pressure, cylinder volume, type of valve gear, receiver capacity, etc, altogether a far from convincing state of affairs. However Fowler was sufficiently encouraged to go ahead with a compound version of the 4–6–2 and in that same month the main details of the design were settled. The closeness of the basic frame layout to the Hughes design will be noted, but obviously the cylinder and valve gear layout had to be different and so was the boiler which conformed to Derby principles. The earlier noted need for a greater coal capacity was ignored by Derby as the standard smaller tender was to be attached! The 2–8–2 design was also prepared in the same detail at the time, but the interesting feature in this case is the larger tender which the reader should keep in mind for the next stage in the design of a Pacific for the LMS. In this Derby design the four-cylinder drive was divided with two sets of outside Walschaerts valve gear operating the four valves, it being realised that separately controlled high- and low-pressure valves were quite unnecessary in British practice. The diameter of the low-pressure outside cylinders would have countered the often made claim that a powerful compound was impossible within the British loading gauge. The high pressure piston valves were to have been 9in diameter and the low pressure 11in. A starting valve was to be incorporated, based on LYR practice, and consisting of a small slide valve in the low-pressure cylinder casting, connected to the reversing shaft so that high-pressure steam would be admitted to the low-pressure cylinders whenever cut-off was less than five percent of maximum in either fore or back gear. The boiler pressure of 240 lb/sq in was the highest yet proposed in Britain. Although the boiler barrel was to be 21ft long, the tubes were to be 17ft, a combustion chamber accounting for the difference. There was a potential source of trouble in the joint of the firebox and barrel where there would have been a very small radius curve at the throatplate, probably leading to poor circulation and wasting of the plates. The small tender would make life difficult for enginemen at times, especially in the winter when strong headwinds were likely, and it certainly inhibited any chance of non-stop London to Glasgow runs. While planning was going on, one of the LYR 4-6-0s, No 10456, was converted to a compound in July 1926, incorporating the Horwich design of starting valve just described. In this conversion the inside low-pressure piston valves were driven by rocker arms of unequal length. No 10456 worked between Crewe and Carlisle, and on test with a 350-ton train showed a saving in coal consumption of nine percent compared with others of the same class when in good condition.

The only reference to the Compound Pacific design contained in LMS locomotive committee minutes was dated 14 March 1926 and referred to the difficulty in overcoming route restrictions; the design was cleared for use between Euston and Glasgow Central, but not via the former Glasgow & South Western Railway line to St Enoch in that city. Nor was it passed to work from Crewe to Manchester, Liverpool or Holyhead, all mentioned as desirable routes if the type were to be a worthwhile proposition. Turntables were another problem at the time and the motive power officer seemed to be decidedly unreceptive to the whole project. So the whole affair passed into limbo as far as the management was concerned, and yet it is clear that some work was done. The author as an engineering apprentice at Crewe Works was told by older hands that they could remember that a start was made but later wondered if they had become confused 25 years after those days by the delay in completing the third of Stanier's Pacifics, to be described in due course. Now he is far from sure, for research has revealed that Derby Works issued construction orders for work to be done in those shops in connection with the building of *five* of the Pacifics at Crewe. Order No 6619 was issued on 23 February 1926 – Order No 6618 was

issued on the same day for similar purposes in connection with *five 2–8–2s* as well! The work was spread between Crewe Works, which was to build the boilers and erect the locomotives, Horwich Works which was to cut the frames, and Derby Works which was to supply many of the fittings. So there was the intention to produce locomotives of both designs, and yet there is no trace of any form of authority being issued by the top management of the LMS nor approval by the company's directors. Significantly there are no gaps in the construction lot lists, no missing order numbers for locomotive construction at Crewe, nor vacant Crewe motion numbers (which were still being allotted at that time) to indicate that anything was done at all! Did Fowler in his enthusiasm for the project exceed his authority? Were orders, motion numbers, etc, removed and all trace obliterated where one would expect to find vacant lots and numbers?

On through the spring and summer of 1926 and into the autumn design work on proposed Pacifics and heavy freight locomotives continued, but already others of influence were setting the stage for a dramatic change, apparently without the knowledge of Fowler. On the motive power side steps had been taken to borrow from the GWR Castle Class 4–6–0 No 5000 *Launceston Castle* and by mid October this locomotive had been used for some weeks between Euston and Crewe handling ordinary revenue-earning trains, later being used also northwards to Carlisle. The results of the locomotive's performance, including trials with a dynomometer car attached, are well known, but even before the measured trials took place between Crewe and Carlisle on 18 and 19 November, all pretence of pushing the Pacific project to fruition was given up when drawing office work ceased on 15 November. The outcome was the design and rapid construction of the 4–6–0 Royal Scot class, first mentioned in locomotive committee minutes on 15 December 1926 when the 1927 Locomotive Programme was recorded, followed by a minute dated 26 January 1927 that an order for 50 had been placed with the North British Locomotive Company. Such was the rapidity of manufacture that the first was ready for inspection by the locomotive committee on 27 July 1927 and with the delivery of all 50 completed by 15 November following the LMS at long last had top-link motive power that gave the company equal standing with the other three main line railways.

All pretence that compounding offered financial advantage was dropped, the day of compound locomotives having already passed as it was abundantly clear that any minimal economy achieved in day-to-day running (better results were obtained by specialised use) were eclipsed by the loss of availability and increased maintenance charges as conditions changed. It is doubtful that the compound Pacific would have been any better than mediocre, having trouble in particular with Derby's specialities, undersized bearings, and short-travel valve gear to inhibit performance. There can be little doubt that the Royal Scot was the better solution at the time, especially as the long-standing agreement over Anglo-Scottish times was still in force. The converted compound, No 10456, continued to work un-noticed until withdrawn in 1936.

The appointment of William Arthur Stanier (later Sir William) was intended to inject into the mechanical affairs of the LMS a new spirit and eliminate the pre-Grouping rivalry that pervaded the Chief Mechanical Engineers' department, workshops and running sheds at almost all levels. It was his job among others to provide modern economical locomotives, the LMS management

The Chief Mechanical Engineer, Mr W. A. (later Sir William) Stanier and members of his staff (left to right) H. Chambers (Derby), R. A. Riddles (Crewe), S. J. Symes (Euston), Stanier, H. P. M. Beames (Derby) and F. A. Lemon (Crewe). *The Railway Gazette.*

being particularly anxious to improve the running of its prestige Anglo-Scottish trains now that the agreement over timings had been cast aside. The need was for a locomotive that could work right through, avoiding the change at Carlisle. The advertised 'non-stop' services in fact stopped there but not in the Citadel station, halting at Kingmoor on the down journey and Upperby on the up to change locomotives – unlike the LNER, there had not been any attempt to provide through corridor tenders.

The choice of a man from another railway, and in particular the Great Western, came as quite a shock to the men of the LMS. Starting on 1 January 1932, his first task was to take stock of a much larger company which in many ways was so vastly different from the GWR, not the least the fact that pre-Grouping rivalries were still strong in several departments, possibly more so in the Chief Mechanical Engineer's than any other. There were those also who recognised the fact that at last someone had the task of producing locomotives recognisable as LMS products and not a carry-over from one of the old companies. The appointment of a senior officer from any other business or firm has always been full of risks – would the newcomer fit in or alienate everyone, would he make sweeping changes, good or bad? Just as Stanier had no experience outside the GWR, so Derby, Crewe and Horwich had no detailed knowledge of the ways of Swindon.

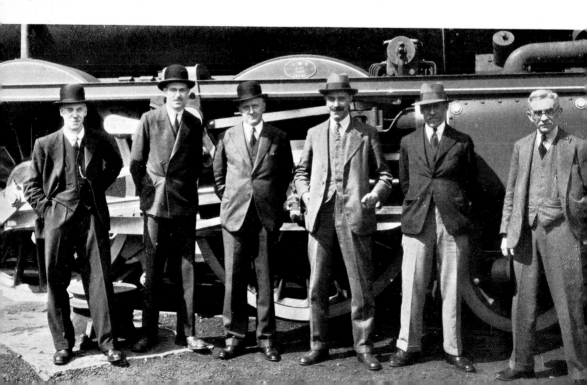

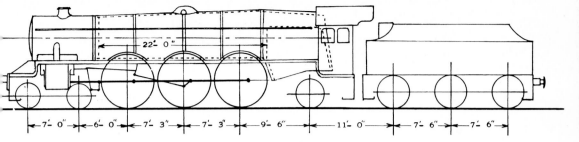

Equally there was the fear that new men would be brought in over those who could reasonably expect promotion in due course, but Stanier avoided so much of this, although a few GWR men made the change, by his personality and during his early years the selection of established LMS men for his immediate subordinates. It goes almost without saying that the design offices were full of rumours at the time, and no doubt technical publications were scoured so that all that was available could be found out about Swindon practice. In view of events and the multitude of design changes applied to the earliest locomotives of Stanier's new classes, the author postulates the opinion that design staff set out to please by producing what they thought to be good copies of Swindon practice and that Stanier accepted them because they conformed to his experience. His greatness came from being able to face reality when shortcomings became apparent and involving everyone who could help in finding and applying the solutions.

Soon a multitude of schemes emerged for new locomotives. At first there was a measure of indecision over three or four cylinders, for the Royal Scot class and the similar but smaller so-called 'Rebuilt Claughton' 4–6–0s (then known almost universally as 'Baby Scots' and later to become officially the Patriot class) were performing very well and Sir Nigel Gresley was continually extolling the virtues of three-cylinder propulsion, building a growing fleet of such locomotives for almost all duties. A whole series of three-cylinder ideas emerged for Pacific, mixed-traffic 4–6–0, 2–8–0 and 2–6–4T types.

Almost without exception a new chief mechanical engineer has been judged by his express passenger locomotives, and their appearance was to give the lay railway press and enthusiasts plenty to discuss as the first of the Pacifics was eagerly awaited. The first major obstacle facing Stanier was that of route clearances; he shrewdly guessed that many places mentioned in locomotive restriction lists had not

Fig 6 Proposed three-cylinder version of Stanier's Pacific schemes prepared in April 1932.
Cylinders (3) 19in x 28in.
Bogie wheels 3ft 3½in; coupled wheels 6ft 9in; bissel truck wheels 4ft 3in.
Grate area 45 sq ft; boiler pressure 250 lb/sq ins; tractive effort 39,700 lb.
Tender wheels 4ft 3in. Coal 9 tons. Water 4,000 gallons.
Estimated weight (locomotive and tender) 104 tons 10 cwt.
Based on information supplied by Mr J. B. Radford.

been checked for many years, even after work done by the civil engineer, and he challenged the latter by sending out for test purposes some of the older 2–6–0 locomotives which had been fitted with 'lead fingers' to create the cross-section profile of his proposed types. At a great many places listed there was in fact sufficient clearance, while at many others only minimal attention needed to permit the new types' passage, leaving many fewer restrictions than ever before. Thus the limitations that had helped to kill off the earlier Pacific proposals were largely swept away.

Top priority was accorded the Anglo-Scottish express locomotive project and there was no doubting the fact that a wide firebox Pacific was the answer. The earliest firm outlines for Stanier Pacifics were produced in April 1932, embodying the following proposals:

No of cylinders	Cylinders		Coupled wheels dia	Boiler pressure lb/sq in	Tractive effort lb	Total weight ton cwt	
	dia in	stroke in					
3	19	28	6ft 9in	250	39,700	104	10
4	16½	28	6ft 9in	250	40,000	104	10

For the three-cylinder version the layout envisaged for the cylinders and motion approximated to that of the Royal Scot Class. Apart from the boiler there was a strong affinity to the Hughes design, particularly with the frames and cab. However, the tender was to be of a design not seen previously on the LMS, but comparing it with that shown for the compound 2–8–2 it will be noted that it was that locomotive's proposed tender resurrected, albeit with an

No 6200 when just completed and not named. (This view appeared in *The Railway Gazette* of 30 June 1933).

increase by one ton in the coal capacity. No wonder it was possible to produce an outline plan so soon after Stanier's arrival, aided by the early appreciation of the direction in which he was likely to head, for the boiler was freely based on Swindon practice, having a tapered barrel and Belpaire firebox. Although the throatplate was sloped there was the inescapable fact that the tubes would have been too long at 22ft. When the final design was approved in late April 1932 there were a number of changes, the four-cylinder version being chosen, with important improvements such as the addition of a short combustion chamber to the firebox and consequent shortening of the tubes and lengthening of the coupled wheelbase from 14ft 6in to 15ft 3in, and reduction of coupled wheel diameter to 6ft 6in. The provisional drawings had shown what appeared to be a stovepipe chimney while the final choice, not taken for some six months, was a capped chimney – the former was nothing more sinister than simplicity in drawing and nothing of intention can be read into it! A curious side effect of the simple chimney shape shown on the earliest plans was the adoption of a stovepipe pattern chimney on a class of 0–4–4T completed in 1932, while another feature shown

Aerial view showing that the tender was as wide as the cab, unlike the similar looking but smaller 'Old Standard' (or Fowler) 3,500-gallon tenders. *The Railway Gazette.*

n some of the schemes, a GWR style safety-valve bonnet, was actually put onto the first of Stanier's second type of locomotive, his version of the 4–6–0, only to be removed immediately when he expressed his disapproval. Such is the wish to please a new chief. Other changes made were the improvement of the cab by enlarging the side windows and extending the roof.

A total of thirteen of this first of Stanier's Pacific classes was built, ordered in two batches in the 1933 and 1935 locomotive building programmes; all were built at Crewe Works. At an early date it was decided to name the locomotives and they became known officially as The Princess Royal Class but more casually, particularly by enginemen, as 'Lizzies'. The third, No 6202, was not named, as it was completed in experimental form as a non-condensing turbine drive locomotive. In fact the decision to do this was taken almost as soon as the 1933 programme was agreed and some £6,000 was allocated for the extra machinery. Much later, in 1952, this locomotive was rebuilt as a conventional four-cylinder reciprocating machine and named *Princess Anne* but tragically its career in this form was extremely short, as it was totally destroyed at Harrow & Wealdstone in the triple collision of October 1952. Otherwise the class remained in full service until withdrawn in 1961–2, although latterly the locomotives had a smaller share of top-link jobs.

With the intention of improving the timings of Anglo-Scottish services in competition with the LNER streamlined trains the LMS held a series of high-speed test runs in 1936 which amply demonstrated the feasibility of an accelerated timetable between London and Glasgow. Although a six-hour schedule was shown to be possible a more cautious timing half-an-hour longer was adopted. Advertised to the public as non-stop, as in past years there were the special stops at Carlisle to change enginemen. Any thoughts of emulating the LNER by using a through gangway for the men to change over en route were dispelled by the need to have as large a coal capacity as possible, for experience had shown that apart from the harder route compared with the East Coast line there were times in strongly adverse weather when every lump was needed and a reduced amount of coal carried would ocasionally lead to locomotives running out of fuel before arriving at the trains' destination – it did indeed happen!

At first a relatively limited enhancement of the Princess Royal design was postulated, some more extreme thoughts such as a water tube firebox being discarded, and the need for streamlining strongly questioned. As scheming progressed, the rapid development of Stanier's principles were taken into account. Those Swindon practices which had proved to be sound on the LMS were further developed and adopted while those that were unsound discarded, refinement of the basic design produced an entirely new class, for which streamlining was adopted. While Stanier's name is rightly attached to this new class he was in fact absent from Britain for almost all of

Right-hand general view of No 6202 (the 'Turbomotive') showing the reverse turbine. *British Rail.*

the time that design work was in progress and it reflects great credit on his principal assistants that such an outstanding product was achieved with minimum direction. The streamlining was far more the result of pressure from publicity officers than technical merit, although some prompting was given by the presentation of two drawings, one streamlined, the other non-streamlined – possibly the addition of a name to the latter, *Lady Godiva*, was a subtle influence.

In July 1936 five additional Pacifics had been added to the 1937 building programme and at the time it was expected that they would be more of the Princess Royals, but as soon as the improved timings were accepted the authority was transferred to the five locomotives planned for the new service. It was not until a shareholders' meeting on 26 February 1937 that the LMS announced its high-speed trains plan and revealed details of the necessary locomotives and coaching stock. The new services started on 5 July 1937 with streamlined trains in a startling new livery of blue-and-silver applied to locomotive, tender, and coaches, but even before

(*top*) No 6220 *Coronation* showing full lining arrangement of the blue streamlined livery. The tender does not have the shrouding that was soon found to be necessary over the coal space. Compare with No 6250 *City of Nottingham* (page 18). *(below)* No 6251 *City of Nottingham* completed without streamlining and in plain wartime black. The tender has no shrouding but still has fairing over the rearward extension. *BR, R. T. Ellis collection.*

they had started it had been decided to bui more of the new class. They became the Prince Coronation class and like the earlier Pacifics h an affectionate name applied by the engineme 'Big Lizzies'. Prior to starting the service the fir locomotive and train set were inspected by th press at Crewe. Stanier welcomed the visitors an the tour was made under the general guidance Mr E. J. H. Lemon, Vice-President of the LM for railway traffic operating and commerci activities. This inspection took place on 28 Ma 1937 but even before, the technical press had see the new train and locomotive, enabling *T Railway Gazette* to publish a full description an general arrangement drawing that same weel Before entering public service a demonstratio run from Euston to Crewe was put on, worked b the first of the class, No 6220 *Coronation*, whic achieved a new world speed record for stean reaching just 114 mph, which was to last b twelve months when its place was taken b *Mallard* of the LNER. The name *Coronation* wa chosen as 1937 was the coronation year of Kin George VI, and the train was titled Coronatio Scot. The service became the high water mark the LMS Anglo-Scottish trains. It proved that th public required faster travel and helped th company to counter possible threats at that tim from internal air services.

Although introduced in publicity as th Princess Coronation Class the company soo dropped 'Princess' so that officially onl Coronation Class was used.

(top) No 6233 *Duchess of Sutherland* of the non-streamlined 1938 batch. *British Rail.* (*below*) No 6256 *Sir William A. Stanier, F.R.S.,* the final version with altered frames at the trailing end and other detail changes. *British Rail.*

The 1938 locomotive building programme contained ten more of the 'Big Lizzies', the first five being streamlined and in a red livery, the other five non-streamlined. The next year's building programme included 20 more and by the outbreak of World War II on 3 September 1939 ten were in service or nearly completed, with work in hand on the next four, all of which were completed as streamliners. Four more followed in 1944, non-streamlined, but the last two of the order were never built, although the boilers intended for them were. The 1940 programme was to have included two 'Super Pacifics' with higher boiler pressure and enlarged superheater, but the war prevented their construction. The remnants of this plan emerged when two of the five non-streamlined locomotives added to the 1946 locomotive programme contained a number of improvements. All 38 were built at Crewe Works between 1937 and 1948, the last being completed by British Railways. All were named, although not in every case having the name originally intended. From 1946 the streamlining was removed.

Not until 1959 was there any challenge to the Coronation Class on the West Coast route, when in that year the first of British Railways' diesel-electric locomotives were allotted in quantity to these services, pending full electrification. The two LMS inspired diesel-electric locomotives, Nos 10000 and 10001, had not made any impact on the Anglo-Scottish services although they had worked some of those trains. Had Britain's railways not been nationalised the story might have been rather different as the two diesels had been built for comparative purposes in 1947–8 and the LMS may well have decided to introduce diesel traction in the early 1950s!

Withdrawal commenced at the end of 1962, and by the end of September 1964 all had ceased working. Now there are but five survivors of the two Stanier Pacific classes in the national collection and private preservationists' hands, or in one case municipal custody.

CHAPTER 2

NUMBERS, NAMES, DIMENSIONS AND LIVERIES

Officially there were only two classes of LMS Pacifics, the Princess Royal Class and the Princess Coronation Class by title, and both 7P in the power classification system (revised to 8P on 1 January 1951). Major variations created in effect four versions of the former and three of the latter.

The range of numbers of the two classes was simply 6200–12 for the thirteen Princess Royal Class and 6220–57 for the thirty-eight Coronation locomotives. There were two orders for the first and four for the latter, being placed as follows:

Date	Construction programme	Number ordered	Running Nos	Estimated cost (£ each)‡
7/1932	1933	3	6200–2	9,210
6/1934	1935	10	6203–12	10,700
7/1936	1937	5	6220–4	10,400
10/1937	1938	10	6225–34	13,800
7/1938	1939	20	6235–54*	12,150
11/1944	1946	5	6253–7	15,170

NOTES:
  ‡ Locomotive and tender (compare with costs given in Tables 1 and 2).
  * Last two of this order cancelled in December 1942.

In addition two 'Super Pacifics' were authorised in June 1939 but they were cancelled in January 1943 as they 'were not so urgently required under wartime conditions'.

All were built at Crewe to the following Lot numbers and Crewe Works Construction Orders:-

Lot No	Crewe order	Locomotive numbers	Remarks
99	371	6200/1	Also Derby order 8254‡
100	371	6202	Also Derby order 8254‡
120	395	6203–12	
138	402	6220–4	Also Derby order 61‡
145	408	6225–34	Also Derby order 311‡
150	414	6235–44	
150	415	6245–52	
184	464	6253–7	

NOTE:
  ‡ Issued for work done by Derby Works staff.

It is perhaps a little surprising that once it had been decided to complete the third of the 1935 Programme as a turbine drive machine that it was not given a distinctive number – 6398, next to the ill-fated *Fury* of 1929, would have been appropriate – but nobody seems to have regarded an entirely separate identity necessary.

When taken into the stock of Britain's nationalised railways four locomotives had the letter M prefixed to the number, denoting London Midland Region (even though one was in Scotland), these being Nos 6206/30/6/57. From March 1948 former LMS numbers were increased by 40000, the individual dates being given in Tables 1 and 2; the last to be built was photographed as No M6257 but was altered to No 46257 before entering service.

After withdrawal from service as a turbine machine on 6 May 1950 the complete rebuilding of No 46202 as a reciprocating locomotive was authorised by the Railway Executive in a minute dated 17 May 1951.

The LMS obtained the approval of the reigning monarch, King George V, to name the prototype locomotives after members of the Royal Family. The Princess Royal was then Colonel-in-Chief of the Royal Scots; curiously this name came in for some sharp criticism in the columns of *The Railway Gazette*, but the choice was defended as being very appropriate in relation to the previous principal passenger express locomotives, the Royal Scot Class. The

No 6207 *Princess Arthur of Connaught* when new. Compare with view of No 6200 for details of motion, valve gear, and shape of firebox throatplate.
BR, R. T. Ellis collection.

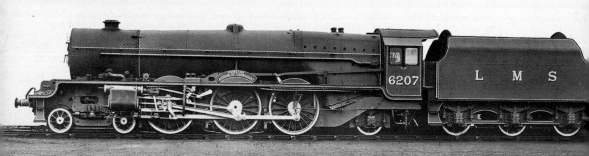

TABLE 1

THE PRINCESS ROYAL CLASS

Loco No	Name	Date New	Date of BR No	New front end	With- drawn
6200	THE PRINCESS ROYAL	7/1933	8/1948	2/1952	11/1962
6201	PRINCESS ELIZABETH	11/1933	8/1948	3/1952	10/1962¢
6202	-	6/1938	3/1949	-	3/1950*
6202	PRINCESS ANNE	8/1952	-	-	5/1954
6203	PRINCESS MARGRET ROSE	7/1935	5/1948	3/1952	10/1962¢
6204	PRINCESS LOUISE	7/1935	4/1948	-	10/1961
6205	PRINCESS VICTORIA	7/1935	5/1948	9/1952	11/1961
6206	PRINCESS MARIE LOUISE	8/1935	11/1948	8/1953	11/1961
6207	PRINCESS ARTHUR OF CONNAUGHT	8/1935	5/1949	1/1954	11/1961
6208	PRINCESS HELENA VICTORIA	8/1935	5/1948	-	10/1962
6209	PRINCESS BEATRICE	8/1935	1/1949	-	9/1962
6210	LADY PATRICIA	9/1935	6/1948	3/1953	10/1961
6211	QUEEN MAUD	9/1935	4/1948	12/1952	10/1961
6212	DUCHESS OF KENT	10/1935	4/1948	-	10/1961

* Stopped working as a turbine drive locomotive 3/1950 but was not withdrawn; rebuilt as No 46202 PRINCESS ANNE in 8/1952, damaged beyond repair in 1952 and finally condemned in 5/1954.

¢ Preserved - see Appendix 4.

The completed costs are recorded as (tender cost in brackets):
Nos 6200/1 £12,567 (£1,951 for No 6200 and £ 1,635 for No 6201),
No 6202 £20,383 (£1,832); £8,875 conversion in 1952,
Nos 6203-12 £8,538 (£1,153) averaged over the whole batch.

rest were named with the exception of No 6202 while it remained in its experimental state, but on rebuilding it was named *Princess Anne*. The names are included in the table of locomotive details. Two need slight amplification: *Lady Patricia* did not show that lady's full title, Lady Patricia Ramsay. Born Princess Patricia of Connaught, she forfeited her royal status at her own request in 1919 when she married a commoner, Lieut. Alexander Ramsay, RN. *Queen Maud* was the wife of the Norwegian monarch.

The initial batch of streamlined locomotives took their names from the fact it was the Coronation year of King George VI. The first became *Coronation*, followed by *Queen Elizabeth* and *Queen Mary*, who was then the Queen Mother, and two more princesses who had not been included in the Princess Royal Class. The 1938 series, both streamlined and non-streamlined, all had the names of duchesses and it was the influence of the latter series that eventually lead to the popular semi-official use of Duchess class to identify the whole series when streamlining had been removed. A complete change was made when 20 city names were chosen for the 1939 order, all being places served by the LMS, although many were inaccessible to the class due to route restrictions. The list was alphabetical in order and would have stayed so had not construction been delayed. The first ten were named as intended, after the cities of Birmingham, Bradford, Bristol, Carlisle, Chester, Coventry, Edinburgh, Glasgow, Lancaster and Leeds, but a change soon took place when the last-named was displaced in favour of the reigning monarch King George VI in April 1941. The selected names for the other

ten were the cities of Leicester, Lichfield, Liverpool, London, Manchester, Nottingham, St Albans, Salford, Sheffield and Stoke-on-Trent; only the third was named as intended, the eight built taking their names from London, Manchester, Liverpool, Leeds, Sheffield, Lichfield, Nottingham and Leicester. When the last five were built the unused names of St Albans, Salford and Stoke-on-Trent were used on Nos 6253, 6257 and 6254 respectively. *City of Hereford* was added to the list (No 6255) – *City of Gloucester* was no doubt ruled out because there

TABLE 2

CORONATION CLASS

Loco No	Name	Date New	Stream- lining removed	Date of BR No	With- drawn
(a) Nos 6220-9 built single chimney and streamlined					
6220	CORONATION	6/1937	9/1946	7/1948	4/1963
6221	QUEEN ELIZABETH	6/1937	5/1946	10/1948	5/1963
6222	QUEEN MARY	6/1937	9/1946	10/1948	10/1963
6223	PRINCESS ALICE	7/1937	8/1946	3/1949	10/1963
6224	PRINCESS ALEXANDRA	7/1937	5/1946	5/1948	10/1963
6225	DUCHESS OF GLOUCESTER	5/1938	2/1947	6/1948	9/1964
6226	DUCHESS OF NORFOLK	5/1938	6/1947	9/1948	9/1964
6227	DUCHESS OF DEVONSHIRE	6/1938	2/1947	5/1948	12/1962
6228	DUCHESS OF RUTLAND	6/1938	7/1947	7/1948	9/1964
6229	DUCHESS OF HAMILTON	9/1938	11/1947	7/1948	2/1964¢
(b) Nos 6230-4 built single chimney but not streamlined					
6230	DUCHESS OF BUCCLEUCH	6/1938	-	5/1948	11/1963
6231	DUCHESS OF ATHOL	6/1938	-	5/1948	12/1962
6232	DUCHESS OF MONTROSE	7/1938	-	5/1948	12/1962
6233	DUCHESS OF SUTHERLAND	7/1938	-	10/1948	2/1964¢
6234	DUCHESS OF ABERCORN	8/1938	-	10/1948	1/1963
(c) Nos 6235-48 built double chimney and streamlined					
6235	CITY OF BIRMINGHAM	7/1939	4/1946	5/1948	9/1964¢
6236	CITY OF BRADFORD	7/1939	12/1947	4/1948	3/1964
6237	CITY OF BRISTOL	8/1939	1/1947	7/1948	9/1964
6238	CITY OF CARLISLE	9/1939	11/1946	3/1949	9/1964
6239	CITY OF CHESTER	9/1939	6/1947	8/1948	9/1964
6240	CITY OF COVENTRY	3/1940	6/1947	6/1948	9/1964
6241	CITY OF EDINBURGH	4/1940	1/1947	5/1948	9/1964
6242	CITY OF GLASGOW	5/1940	3/1947	5/1948	10/1963
6243	CITY OF LANCASTER	6/1940	5/1949	4/1948	9/1964
6244	CITY OF LEEDS **	7/1940	8/1947	8/1948	9/1964
6245	CITY OF LONDON	6/1943	8/1947	8/1948	9/1964
6246	CITY OF MANCHESTER	8/1943	9/1946	11/1948	1/1963
6247	CITY OF LIVERPOOL	9/1943	5/1947	11/1948	5/1963
6248	CITY OF LEEDS	10/1943	12/1946	3/1949	9/1964
(d) Nos 6249-57 built with double chimney but not streamlined					
6249	CITY OF SHEFFIELD	4/1944	-	4/1948	11/1963
6250	CITY OF LICHFIELD	5/1944	-	2/1949	9/1964
6251	CITY OF NOTTINGHAM	6/1944	-	5/1948	9/1964
6252	CITY OF LEICESTER	6/1944	-	4/1949	5/1963
6253	CITY OF ST. ALBANS	9/1946	-	9/1949	1/1963
6254	CITY OF STOKE-ON-TRENT	9/1946	-	7/1949	9/1964
6255	CITY OF HEREFORD	10/1946	-	6/1949	9/1964
6256	SIR WILLIAM A. STANIER, F.R.S.	12/1947	-	5/1948	10/1964
6257	CITY OF SALFORD	2/1948‡	-	5/1948	9/1964

¢ Preserved - see Appendix 4.

** Renamed KING GEORGE VI 4/1941.

‡ Not released to traffic until 5/1948.

Nos 6220 and 6229 exchanged identities from 1/1939 until 3/1942.

Nos 6220-9 and 6235-48 had smoke deflectors fitted when the streamlining was removed.

Nos 6220-34 had double chimneys fitted at the following dates:-

6220	12/1944	6223	11/1941	6226	7/1942	6229	4/1943	6232	1/1943
6221	11/1940	6224	5/1940	6227	12/1940	6230	10/1940	6233	3/1941
6222	8/1943	6225	6/1943	6228	9/1940	6231	6/1940	6234	2/1940

Nos 6220-9 and 6235-48 had the sloping front of the smokeboxes replaced at the following dates:-

6220	2/1957	6225	1/1955	6235	7/1952	6240	5/1957	6245	12/1957
6221	9/1952	6226	11/1955	6236	11/1953	6241	2/1958	6246	5/1960
6222	8/1953	6227	5/1953	6237	5/1956	6242	11/1953	6247	5/1958
6223	8/1955	6228	1/1957	6238	10/1953	6243	11/1958	6248	6/1958
6224	10/1954	6229	2/1957	6239	2/1957	6244	7/1953		

Nos 6230-4 and 6249-52 had smoke deflectors fitted at the following dates:-

6230	9/1946	6232	2/1945	6234	9/1946	6250	3/1946	6252	3/1945
6231	9/1946	6233	9/1946	6249	11/1946	6251	8/1946		

(Nos 6253-7 were fitted with smoke deflectors when new).

The completed costs are recorded as, averaged in batches (tender cost in brackets):

Nos 6220-4	£11,813 (£1,556)	No 6247	£9,037 (£1,670)
Nos 6225-9	£10,136 (£1,601)	No 6248	£9,445 (£1,670)
Nos 6230-4	£9,585 (£1,509)	Nos 6249-52	£10,069 (£1,670)
Nos 6235-44	£9,437 (£1,549)	Nos 6253-5	£15,460 **
No 6245	£9,324 (£1,670)	Nos 6256/7	£18,248 (£3,163)
No 6246	£10,182 (£1,670)		

** Not quoted but possibly £3,163.

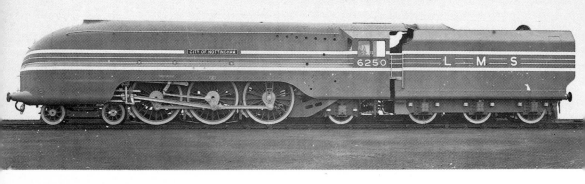

A red streamliner that never was! One of the 1939 batch painted and numbered as No 6250 *City of Nottingham*, the correct name in the planned sequence of naming. Note shrouding now fitted to tender – compare with photograph of No 6220 *Coronation. Crown Copyright, courtesy National Railway Museum.*

was already No 6225 *Duchess of Gloucester* in the class. Right at the end of the existence of the LMS the opportunity was taken to honour the man responsible for the dramatic change that took place in the motive power of the company when No 6256 was named *Sir William A. Stanier F.R.S.* at a special ceremony at Euston on 17 December 1947. Stanier was unique among British locomotive engineers in becoming a Fellow of the Royal Society – George Stephenson, the only other railway engineer so honoured, was responsible for railway building as well as establishing the basic principles of the steam locomotive.

Naming ceremonies for some of those named after cities were held as follows:-

6235 *City of Birmingham*	20 Mar., 1945
6240 *City of Coventry*	6 Nov., 1945
6245 *City of London*	20 July, 1943
6246 *City of Manchester*	3 Sept., 1943
6248 *City of Leeds*	2 Dec., 1943
6249 *City of Sheffield*	1 Nov., 1944
6250 *City of Lichfield*	20 Jun., 1944
6251 *City of Nottingham*	4 Oct., 1945
6252 *City of Leicester*	9 Oct., 1944
6254 *City of Stoke-on-Trent*	20 Sept., 1946
46257 *City of Salford*	3 Jun., 1948

Apart from No 6248 which was named at Euston, all visited the city honoured, thus taking them to places well outside their normal routes. The ceremony for No 6246 was held at Manchester Victoria station rather than London Road (nowadays Piccadilly). Manchester Exchange was the venue when 46257 was named. No 6251 immediately after the ceremony became derailed

on leaving the Lincoln end of Nottingham station, causing considerable delays. No 6249 was presented with a set of stainless steel nameplates, manufactured by one of the Sheffield steel firms, Firth-Vickers Stainless Steels Ltd, which were fitted about two months after the ceremony. No 6254 could get to Stoke-on-Trent only from Norton Bridge, being prohibited from any other route into the city. In addition to their nameplates Nos 6235/40/54 had the city arms on plaques affixed above the plates. No 6220 *Coronation* was adorned with a crown above each nameplate.

There was a curious twist to the change in the order of naming of the 'cities' batch. One of the streamliners was used for a series of photographs depicting each one, numbers and names being altered to suit, which created the anomaly of not only having the wrong number/name combination but also illustrations of streamlined 'cities' that never were!

TABLE 3
LOCOMOTIVE DIMENSIONS

Cylinders (4)	16½in X 28in	Nos 6200/1/3-12
	16½in X 28in	Nos 6202 (rebuilt), 6220-57
Bogie wheels	3ft 0in	
Coupled wheels	6ft 6in	Nos 6200-12
	6ft 9in	Nos 6220-57
Trailing wheels	3ft 9in	
Boiler type	1	Nos 6200-12
(see Table 4)	1X	Nos 6220-57
Boiler pressure	250 lbs/sq in	
Maximum axle load	22 tons 10 cwt	Nos 6200/1/3-12
	23 tons 6 cwt	No 6202 (Turbomotive)
	22 tons 4 cwt	No 6202 (rebuilt)
	22 tons 10 cwt	Nos 6220-9/35-48 (streamlined)
	22 tons 9 cwt	Nos 6220-55 (non-streamlined)
	22 tons 15 cwt	Nos 6256/7
Adhesive weight	67 tons 10 cwt	Nos 6200/1/3-12
	68 tons 19 cwt	No 6202 (Turbomotive)
	66 tons 10 cwt	No 6202 (rebuilt)
	67 tons 2 cwt	Nos 6220-9/35-48 (streamlined)
	66 tons 19 cwt	Nos 6220-55 (non-streamlined)
	68 tons 5 cwt	Nos 6256/7
Weight empty	94 tons 7 cwt	Nos 6200/1/3-12
	100 tons 8 cwt	No 6202 (Turbomotive)
	95 tons 1 cwt	No 6202 (rebuilt)
	98 tons 7 cwt	Nos 6220-9/35-48 (streamlined)
	95 tons 10 cwt	Nos 6220-55 (non-streamlined)
	98 tons 15 cwt	Nos 6256/7
Weight working order	104 tons 10 cwt‡	Nos 6200/1/3-12
	110 tons 11 cwt‡	No 6202 (Turbomotive)
	105 tons 4 cwt	No 6202 (rebuilt)
	108 tons 2 cwt	Nos 6220-9/35-48 (streamlined)
	105 tons 5 cwt	Nos 6220-55 (non-streamlined)
	108 tons 10 cwt	Nos 6256/7
Tractive effort	40,300 lbs	Nos 6200/1/3-12
	41,538 lbs	No 6202 (rebuilt)
	40,000 lbs	Nos 6220-57

‡ Weight as shown on third engine diagram issued; recorded as 109 tons 0 cwt on initial diagram.

TABLE 4

BOILER DIMENSIONS

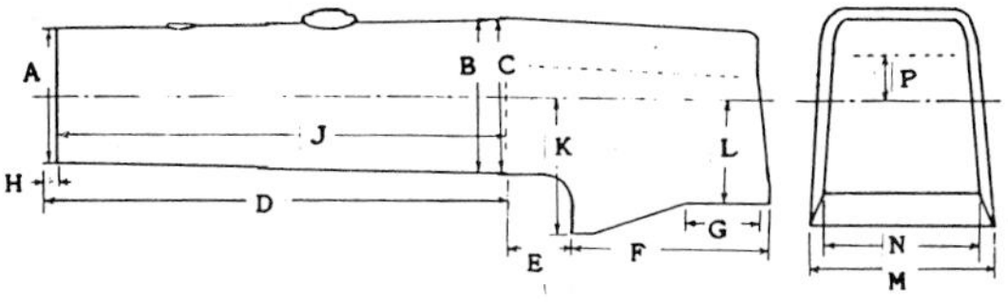

DIMENSION AS INDICATED ON CHART	BOILER TYPE 1 6048-50	BOILER TYPE 1 others	BOILER TYPE 1X all
	ft in	ft in	ft in
A outside diameter of front of barrel	5 8⅜	5 8⅜	5 8⅜
B outside diameter of back of barrel	6 3	6 3	6 5½
C outside diameter joint ring barrel/firebox	6 4¾	-	-
D length of barrel (including joint ring)	20 7 3/16	19 10 11/16	19 10 11/16
E length of throatplate	2 7	3 3½	3 3 11/16
F length of firebox at foundation ring	8 6	8 6	8 6
G length of flat section of grate (internally from backplate)	2 11½	2 11½	2 11 9/16
H recess of tubeplate (including 13/16in thickness of tubeplate)	0 7⅛	0 7⅛	0 7 13/16
J tube length (between tubeplates)	20 9	19 3	19 3
K depth of firebox at throatplate (from centre line)	5 6⅞	5 6⅞	5 8⅞
L depth of firebox at firedoor plate (from centre line)	4 2⅞	4 2⅞	4 4⅞
M width of firebox at throatplate	7 1	6 10¾	6 11 1/16
N width of firebox at firedoor plate	6 1	6 2⅞	6 2 23/32
P internal height of crown at throatplate (from centre line)	1 2⅜	1 2⅜	1 4

For tube arrangements and heating surfaces of Type 1 boilers see Tables 5 and 6; the following dimensions are applicable to the Type 1X boiler:

Tubes	No/diameter	129/2⅜in and 40/5⅛in
Heating surface	tubes firebox	2,577 sq ft 230 sq ft - 2,807 sq ft
Superheater (40 elements, 1in triple)		856 sq ft (13 swg) 830 sq ft (11 swg) 822 sq ft (10 swg)
Superheater (5P4 elements on Nos 6256/7 when new)		979 sq ft

TABLE 5

BOILER TYPE 1 TUBE ARRANGEMENTS

(THE PRINCESS ROYAL CLASS)

(a) Boiler Nos 6048-50 (built to order B371):

Boiler No	Dome fitted	Tube arrangement (No/diam) and heating surface (sq ft)				
		170/2¼in 16/5⅛in 2523	168/2¼in 16/5⅛in 2499	119/2⅜in 32/5⅛in 2425	110/2¼in 32/5⅛in 2240	110/2⅜in 32/5⅛in 2310
6048	10/35	New	*/34	10/35	-	-
6049	6/36	New	*/34	6/36	-	-
6050	11/52	-	-	-	New	*/40

(b) Boiler Nos 9100-9 (built to order B395) and 9235 (built to spare order BS1/15):

Boiler No	Dome fitted	Tube arrangement (No/diam) and heating surface (sq ft)				
		112/2¼in 32/5⅛in 2097	112/2⅜in 32/5⅛in 2167	141/2¼in 24/5⅛in 2218	141/2⅜in 24/5⅛in 2307	123/2⅜in 32/5⅛in 2299
9100	12/52	New	5/39	-	-	‡
9101	6/55	-	-	New	11/38	3/44
9102	12/55	-	-	New	2/38	2/51
9103	3/53	-	-	New	3/38	11/43
9104	2/56	-	-	New	8/37	9/50
9105	1/52	New	10/37	-	-	‡
9106	12/56	New	10/38	-	-	10/47
9107	12/52	New	8/39*	-	-	10/45
9108	12/55	New	4/38	-	-	9/50
9109	1/54	New	4/38	-	-	10/44
9235	9/52	New	8/39*	-	-	9/52

(c) Boiler No 9236 (built to spare order BS1/15):

Boiler No	Dome fitted	Tube arrangement (No/diam) and heating surface (sq ft)	
		81/2¼in 40/5⅛in 1951	101/2⅜in 40/5⅛in 2232
9236	New	New	5/52

* Month not known or uncertain.

‡ Nos 9100/5 apparently never altered to this arrangement.

TABLE 6

BOILER TYPE 1 SUPERHEATER DETAILS

(THE PRINCESS ROYAL CLASS)

Element details and heating surface (sq ft):

No of elements	16	32	24	32	32	32	32	40	40	40	40
Diameter	1⅜in	1¼in	1¼in	1¼in	1¼in	1¼in	1½in	1in	1in	1in	1¼in
swg	11	13	11	11	11	11	9	11	**	11	9
Boiler Nos											
6048/9	370	-	-	-	623	598	586	-	-	-	-
6050	-	-	-	594	623	598	586	-	-	-	-
9100	-	653	-	-	623	598	586	-	-	-	-
9101-4	-	-	467	-	-	598	586	-	-	-	-
9105-9 ≠	-	≠	-	-	623	598	586	-	-	-	-
9235	-	-	-	-	623	598	586	-	-	-	-
9236 ‡	-	-	-	-	-	-	-	577	832	540	720

** Triple elements.

≠ Recorded as 653 sq ft on the engine diagram issued in June 1935, but reduced to 623 sq ft on a re-issue of September 1935; therefore the first mentioned may not have been used.

‡ The first diagram for the rebuilding of No 6202 shows 40 1½in/10swg elements having a heating surface of 752 sq ft; these elements were not used.

NOTES: The 1¼in /11swg elements with 623 sq ft dated from 1935,
The 1¼in /11swg elements with 598 sq ft dated from about 1946,
The 1½in / 9swg elements with 586 sq ft dated from 1952.

The successive arrangements for boiler No 9236 date from 1936, 1938, 1946 and 1952 respectively.

Throughout their existence the basic dimensions changed little, especially those of 'Big Lizzies'. The 'Lizzies' were affected by a seemingly endless variety of boiler tube and superheater re-arrangements, so producing a variety of heating surfaces which so easily caused confusion. The basic boiler dimensions are given in Table 4 and the tube and superheater figures in Tables 5 and 6. Superheater values were changed when the specifications of the elements were altered, either their outside diameter or their thickness (measured in swg) – the lower the number of the swg, the thicker the tube wall and therefore the smaller the heating surface because of the reduced internal diameter. This is shown best by the change of superheating surface of the 'Big Lizzies' where the element diameter remained at 1in and the successive swg of the elements was 13, 11, and 10, giving heating surface figures of 856, 830, and 822. It is perhaps worth mentioning that the method of calculating the heating surface of superheaters had been standardised by the Association of Locomotive Engineers in 1914, using the internal diameter of the element and disregarding the return bends and connection to the superheater header outside the large tubes where any heating effect of the gases was utterly minimal.

Several forms of livery were applied to both classes, the Coronations having no fewer than eleven variations during an existence of just over 27 years!

All the 'Lizzies' started in LMS crimson lake with full lining and 12in numerals. The insignia was gold, shaded black, with 14in serif lettering. Some were turned out with the 1936 style gold

TABLE 7
LMS PACIFIC LIVERIES

Loco No	First Livery	Wartime black	Exptl grey	LMS black	BR black	BR blue	BR green	BR red
6200	Red	-	-	9/47	-	-	4/52	5/58
6201	Red	-	-	8/47	2/48	-	4/52	-
6202	Red	-	-	5/47	3/49	-	8/52	-
6203	Red	-	-	12/47	-	-	3/52	-
6204	Red	-	-	-	-	-	5/52	8/58
6205	Red	-	-	-	11/48*	-	9/52	-
6206	Red	-	-	2/48	-	11/50	8/53*	-
6207	Red	-	-	-	5/49	-	12/51	5/58
6208	Red	-	-	-	-	9/50	11/52	9/58
6209	Red	-	-	-	5/48	-	9/51	-
6210	Red	-	-	8/47	-	5/50*	3/53*	-
6211	Red	-	-	2/47	6/49*	-	12/52*	-
6212	Red	-	-	-	4/49	-	11/52*	-
6220	Blue	3/44	-	10/46	-	1/50	8/52	-
6221	Blue	8/44	-	7/46	-	2/50*	1/52	-
6222	Blue	10/44	-	5/46	-	9/50*	12/52	-
6223	Blue	2/44	-	8/46	-	3/50	9/52	-
6224	Blue	10/44	-	7/46	-	5/48‡	4/52	-
6225	Red	4/44	-	3/47	-	2/50	2/53	8/58
6226	Red	*/44	-	6/47	11/48	5/49	4/51*	11/58
6227	Red	1/44	-	3/47	-	5/48‡	5/53	-
6228	Red	4/44	-	11/47	-	8/50	8/55	6/58
6229	Red	8/43*	-	12/47	-	1/50	3/52	9/58
6230	Red	-	-	9/46	-	5/48‡	3/52	-
6231	Red	8/45*	-	9/46	-	5/48‡	11/53	-
6232	Red	2/45	-	9/47	-	-	11/51*	-
6233	Red	-	-	9/46	-	-	12/52*	-
6234	Red	-	3/46	-	-	5/48‡	1/52	-
6235	Red	3/43	-	4/46	-	10/50*	4/53	-
6236	Red	4/44	-	12/47	-	-	8/55	7/58
6237	Red	8/43*	-	2/47	-	8/49*	8/52*	-
6238	Red	*/43	-	8/46	3/49	-	10/53	6/58
6239	Red	3/44*	-	9/47	-	6/50*	7/54*	-
6240	Red	11/45	-	7/47	-	1/50	9/54*	7/58
6241	Red	5/43*	-	2/47	-	5/48‡	4/53*	-
6242	Red	5/44	-	5/47	-	8/49	11/53	-
6243	Red	1/44	-	-	-	6/49	1/54*	10/58
6244	Red	1/44	-	8/47	-	9/48‡	5/53	10/58
6245	Black	New	-	11/47	-	-	4/53	12/57
6246	Black	New	-	11/46	11/48	-	5/53*	10/58
6247	Black	New	-	2/47	-	-	1/54*	5/58
6248	Black	New	-	1/47	3/49	-	8/53*	6/58
6249	Black	New	-	11/46	-	8/50*	1/53*	-
6250	Black	New	-	7/47	-	3/50*	9/52*	-
6251	Black	New	-	6/47	4/49	-	10/51*	11/58
6252	Black	New	-	11/46*	3/49	*/50*	1/54*	-
6253	Black	-	-	New	-	-	10/53*	-
6254	Black	-	-	New	-	8/50*	1/53*	9/58
6255	Black	-	-	New	-	6/50	4/53	-
6256	Black	-	-	New	11/48	3/51*	5/54*	5/58
6257	Black	-	-	New	-	New	11/52*	-

* Probably into service a month or two later (also month not known in certain cases).

‡ Experimental blue livery at first painting.

Nos 46206/12/36/56/7 ran with tenders lettered BRITISH RAILWAYS.

Contrast in liveries, red No 6227 *Duchess of Devonshire* and blue No 6223 *Princess Alice* at Polmadie shed on 29 August 1938. *T. G. Hepburn/Rail Archive Stephenson.*

sans-serif insignia, having red shading, Nos 6204/6/10/2 certainly appearing so. This style was discarded in 1937, apart from the use of red shading which all of the class acquired, as far as can be checked. After World War II the LMS adopted a black livery, with maroon-and-straw lining and insignia, but of the thirteen locomotives only Nos 6200–3/6/10/1 had it applied, all of the others remaining in red at the time. Early in 1948 British Railways started to use a plain black livery with LNWR-style lining and Nos 46201/2/5/7/9/11/2 were so treated; there seems to be no record of Nos 46204 and 46208 appearing in black. In 1950 it was decided to adopt a blue livery for express passenger classes, a few locomotives having been in various shades of blue since 1948. Three 'Lizzies' were so painted, Nos 46206/8/10, but it failed to please, acquiring (in memory) a very dull appearance within a short time. The GWR-style Brunswick green adopted for other express passenger classes was therefore chosen as a replacement for the blue and all of the class acquired the green lined livery in 1951–3. Finally, as a publicity move, four were restored to their first LMS livery, two complete with LMS style lining (Nos 46200 and 46207) and the other two with BR lining (No 46204, which was later reported to be altered to LMS style lining, and No 46208).

Of the eleven livery forms used on the 'Big Lizzies' only one was applied to the whole class, when for just over two years from August 1955 to December 1957 all were in the British Railways lined green. The first streamliners appeared in an attractive blue with four silver bands along the

bodyside meeting in a 'V' just above the front drawhook. Of these bands the two outer were much wider than the inner pair and all four were lined with a darker blue band. Wheels were dark blue, tyres and motion highly polished. The nameplates had silver letters and rims with a blue background. The next five streamliners, Nos 6225–9, had crimson lake instead of blue, the bands being gold instead of silver; the lining was black with a very thin vermilion line between the gold and black. The nameplate background was crimson lake and this time the wheels were black. When No 6229 was sent to America in the guise of No 6220 it stayed in this livery and the visual consequence was that a blue No 6229 was running in this country. Ten more were finished in red and gold despite the start of World War II before all had entered service, these being Nos 6235–44. Of the pre-war locomotives the non-streamliners Nos 6230–4 alone appeared in the standard LMS crimson lake, having gold lining,

(*top*) No 6235 *City of Birmingham* in plain black. The upper shrouding has been removed from the tender. *British Rail.*

(*above*) No 46229 *Duchess of Hamilton* after removal of the streamlining and turned out in the post-War LMS lined black. The open front end of the platforms was adopted on de-streamlining to save time at examinations when piston valves had to be withdrawn. Note serif style smokebox number plate. *British Rail.*

edged with vermilion instead of straw, so strictly speaking even they were non-standard.

From 1943 plain black became the livery and four streamliners, Nos 6245–8, appeared so, followed by the last four, Nos 6249–52, as black non-streamliners. The plain black was applied at wartime overhauls to all but Nos 6230/3/4. While deciding on the post-war livery the LMS tried out grey paint on No 6234 in March 1946; this had maroon and straw lining. However, black was chosen as described for the 'Lizzies' and in addition to Nos 6253–6 which had it from new all

No 46230 *Duchess of Buccleuch* in the British Railways blue livery. Unlike the formerly streamlined locomotives the full platforms remained at the front end. The smokebox number plate has gill sans figures. *British Rail.*

but Nos 6234 and 6243 were changed to it in 1946–7. No 46257 appeared in the BR black with LNWR lining in 1948, joined by another seven in that year and 1949. At the same time blue livery was tried on Nos 6224/30/1/4/41/4 but it was a somewhat darker shade than that generally adopted in 1950 and applied to most of the class before the change to green began in 1951. The blue livery had black-and-white lining and everything below the platforms was black, except that the cylinders and running plate angles were lined. The nameplates were black with polished letters. With the green livery orange-and-black lining was applied.

As with the Princess Royal Class a final change was made in 1957–8 when sixteen Coronations were given the LMS-style crimson lake livery, although British Railways called it maroon. Some had BR-style lining, but most had or were altered to LMS-style lining. Nameplates were black with polished lettering and rims; for the first time under British Railways ownership lining was extended to include footsteps and tender framing. The last working locomotive of the

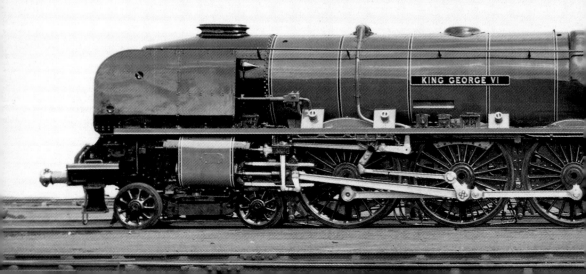

class, No 46256, was in this livery at withdrawal. Table 7 details livery changes from 1943 onwards, starting with the application of the plain wartime black.

A mundane but somewhat startling change to the livery of the last survivors was made right at the end of their working life when in readiness for September 1964 it was ordered that a broad diagonal stripe be painted across the cabsides, broken only by the numerals. This was done to warn enginemen and others that the class was to be prohibited south of Crewe under the newly installed ac overhead electrification which compared with the sections between Crewe and Manchester and Liverpool had reduced clearances above the loading gauge. The 'Big Lizzies' and several other classes by their height fouled the new standard electrical clearance below the wire. Also in connection with the forthcoming electrification, locomotives had been adorned with small rectangular electrification warning plates at points where they were visible to staff when climbing up to or standing on any part of the locomotive or tender where there was a risk of coming into contact with the overhead line – the same plate continues in use on British Railways rolling stock.

Of the preserved locomotives only No 46235 *City of Birmingham* has remained in the livery in which it was withdrawn, being in the lined green. The other four preserved, Nos 6201/3/29/33, are in red but with varying degrees of accuracy, particularly the lining and insignia, which do not entirely agree with any condition in which they ran.

The cabside stripe adopted in 1964 to indicate that the locomotive was prohibited from working south of Crewe under the overhead electrified line. *Alec Swain.*

No 46244 *King George VI* in the British Railways lined green livery, showing the original 'lion-and-wheel' tender emblem. *British Rail.*

CHAPTER 3

THE PRINCESS ROYAL CLASS – THE FIRST TWO

In construction and in details the new Pacifics set a completely new standard for the LMS. At the time of entry into service the technical railway press described the design in detail and gave due credit to the company's Derby drawing office, adding that the work was done under the instructions of Mr Stanier. The following technical description is that of the first two, Nos 6200 and 6201, and the variations that appeared with Nos 6203–12 are added afterwards. A description of the totally different transmission of No 6202, the 'Turbomotive' follows in Chapter 4.

The immediate impression was that of a long, low machine but the locomotives were full height – it was the extended trailing end and wide firebox that created the impression of length. In so many respects it was quickly apparent that the design owed much to Swindon and GWR practice, so much so that it was considered to be very much the shape of a Great Western Pacific had such a type appeared at the time. There were so many GWR characteristics that it seemed to many that one era had vanished almost overnight, to be replaced by one which was totally alien to all that was to be seen as LMS locomotive practice. This was largely true, but as will be revealed in later chapters the new master was not so dogmatic

in his views as to be blind to faults or unsuitable designs when experience dictated that change was needed.

Locomotives with four-cylinder drive were not new to the LMS, the company having acquired 130 of the LNWR Claughton class 4–6–0s and one former Glasgow & South Western Railway 4–4–0 so fitted. On both classes all four cylinders drove the leading coupled axle, but for the 'Lizzies' the divided drive which was so successful on the GWR was adopted. Thus the outside cylinders, inclined at 1 in 35, were approximately central over the trailing bogie wheels, while the inside pair which were horizontal lay almost centrally over the leading wheels, a disposition that helped to equalise cylinder weight over the bogie wheelbase. Steam was distributed to the cylinders by 8in diameter piston valves, having a travel of $7\frac{1}{4}$in. The steam ports from the valve chambers to the cylinders were straight and because the valves had inside admission the two separate exhaust passages for the inside cylinders were carried over the top of the steamchest and merged together at the rear of these cylinders where the front smokebox saddle formed the upper part of the casting. The exhaust ports for the outside cylinders were taken through the main frame to a branch casting which formed a separate saddle for the smokebox at its centre line. A departure from Derby practice was

No 6200 ready for release from Crewe Locomotive Works. Note that the name at this stage was *Princess Royal*. LMS, *R. T. Ellis collection*.

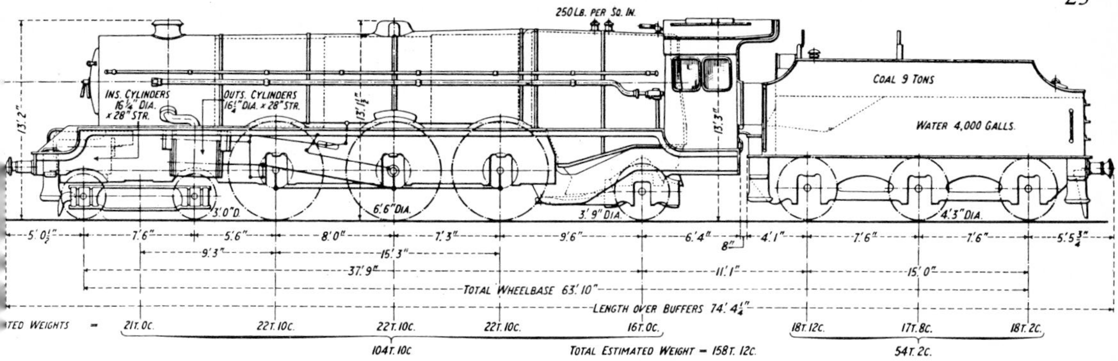
250 LB. PER SQ. IN.
INS. CYLINDERS 16¼" DIA. x 28" STR.
OUTS. CYLINDERS 16¼" DIA. x 28" STR.
COAL 9 TONS
WATER 4,000 GALLS.
13'2"
13'3"
3'0"D.
6'6" DIA.
3'9" DIA.
4'3" DIA.
5'0½"
7'6"
5'6"
8'0"
7'3"
9'6"
6'4"
8"
4'1"
7'6"
7'6"
5'5¾"
9'3"
15'3"
37'9"
11'1"
15'0"
TOTAL WHEELBASE 63'10"
LENGTH OVER BUFFERS 74'4¼"
TED WEIGHTS - 21T.0C. 22T.10C. 22T.10C. 22T.10C. 16T.0C. 18T.12C. 17T.8C. 18T.2C.
104T.10C
TOTAL ESTIMATED WEIGHT - 158T.12C.
54T.2C.

Fig 7 Princess Royal class Nos 6200 and 6201. *The Railway Gazette.*

the omission of Fowler-Anderson cylinder by-pass valves which were designed to admit air to both sides of a piston when drifting; it was accepted that by placing the valve gear at 45 percent cut-off when coasting that excessive compression was avoided and that any resultant trouble at connecting rod big-ends just would not occur. Drawings show that these by-pass valves were intended and the cylinders were indeed cast with the internal passages needed for this device. LMS standard cylinder drain cocks were fitted, but Stanier evidently regarded the existing cylinder compression valves as oversize, fitting a smaller type instead. Cylinder clearance volume was 9.4 percent of the swept volume. There was a 16-feed mechanical lubricator on the left side of the locomotive, supplying superheater grade oil to the eight piston valve heads, the four cylinder barrels and four piston rod packings. The mechanical lubricator on the right-hand side supplied engine grade oil to the four piston valve guide spindle bushes. These bushes, which had only exhaust steam in contact with them, were made of phosphor bronze lined with white metal, their inside diameter being 1⅞ and the length almost 7¾in. The oil supply from the left-hand lubricator to the piston valve heads and the cylinder barrels was atomised by means of an atomiser jet just before the delivery point; in the case of the valves the atomised oil was passed into annular spaces provided in the cylinder casting behind the liners before entry into the steamchests through six holes, spaced equally around the valve liners so that the whole surface of the piston valve heads was fully lubricated. The position of these apertures was such that the atomised oil entered on the live steam side to be carried by the natural flow of the steam through the valve chests and into the cylinders.

The leading particulars of the valve gear are set out in Table 8.

TABLE 8
VALVE MOTION PARTICULARS

Class	Princess Royal				Coronation
Motion	Inside		Outside		All
Locomotive numbers	6200/1	6203-12	6200/1	6203-12	6220-57
Throw of eccentrics	9in	9in	9in	16½in	15in
Angle of eccentrics	98°15'	98°15'	98°	92°40'	92°40'
Maximum travel (fore gear)	7 9/32in	7 5/16in	7 9/32in	7¼in	7 1/32in
Maximum travel (back gear)	7 1/16in	6⅞in	7 1/16in	6 15/16in	6¾in
Lead	¼in	¼in	¼in	¼in	1/16in
Steam lap	1¾in	1¾in	1¾in	1¾in	1¾in
Exhaust clearance	Line-and-line		Line-and-line		1/16in
Maximum cut-off	73%	73%	73%	73%	75%

Between centres, the inside and outside connecting rods were 8ft 6½in and 9ft 0in in length respectively, the latter fluted, the former of plain rectangular section. The coupling rods were also of plain rectangular section and all these rods were produced from a high manganese molybdenum steel. The big-ends of the outside rods had solid bushes pressed into the butt ends of the rods with white-metal lining. The big-ends of the inside rods were forked with split brasses retained by a driven cotter, quite different from the strap type previously used on the LMS. The coupling and connecting rods were provided with bronze lubricating rings designed to reduce side wear. In the design and layout of the valve gear and motion special attention was given to lubrication needs, especially as the locomotives were intended to perform runs of 400 miles.

Each piston valve head was 3½in wide over the six narrow rings (¼in wide and 5/16in deep) and conformed to newly-adopted LMS practice. Stanier did not enforce use of the Swindon pattern of valve head, possibly seeing that it was in no way superior. There was the convincing fact recently proven on the LMS that with narrow rings there was not the excessive rise in steam consumption when valve rings of the wide type that had been in use became due for renewal. Piston heads were of the box type with plain end surfaces and three rings ($\frac{5}{16}$in wide and $\frac{9}{16}$in deep) were fitted. The head was screwed onto the piston rod, the threads of both being six per inch and tapered, the fitting allowance on the head ensuring that it was held securely. The piston rod was $3\frac{1}{4}$in in diameter and was held in the crosshead by a cotter, tapered at 1 in 48, which when driven home forced the tapered end (1 in 18) into the similarly tapered socket in the crosshead with a loading of 30 tons. This was done so that the distance between piston heads and cylinder covers was no more than a $\frac{1}{4}$in, thereby reducing the clearance volume. Air relief valves (often called 'snifters' or anti-vacuum valves) were fitted to each cylinder, and when coasting they lifted off their seats to destroy the vacuum otherwise created in the steam chests and cylinders. This arrangement was intended to keep down carbonisation, a problem that had been quite difficult to deal with on superheated locomotives.

Separate Walschaerts valve gear was provided for each cylinder, for at that time it was considered that to drive one valve from another by means of a rocking lever would result in unequal steam distribution, although Stanier was well acquainted with two sets of valve gear driving four valves on GWR four-cylinder locomotives. Like GWR locomotives a crosshead-driven vacuum pump was fitted, attached to the left-hand outside slide bar. The reversing screw, standing on a pedestal in the cab, was connected to the weightbar shaft by a two-part bridle rod, such was the distance between them. At the intermediate point a double-armed shaft, resting on bearings placed on the left-hand platform just to the rear of the trailing coupled wheel splasher, joined the two portions. The weighbar shaft was placed just in front of the centre coupled wheels and was connected directly to the outside valve gear, but there had to be an intermediate bridle rod to reach a second weighbar entirely within the frames for the inside motion. This additional rod lay on the left side of the locomotive. The principal weighbar shaft was counterbalanced with a helical spring, placed along the centre line of the locomotive. Due to the wide firebox it was necessary to offset the bridle rod (another reason for the intermediate double armed shaft) further out than customary and insert a set of gear wheels so that the reverser could stand in its usual place and have ample clearance at the cab side for its

handle; this was not actually novel on the LMS as the Garratts had a similar arrangement.

Slidebars, resembling strongly the GWR pattern, rested at the open end on the outside motion brackets, which compared with later locomotives of the class were unobtrusively attached to the frames behind the motion, or the inside motion plate, being supported at the cylinder end by brackets on the covers, two fixing bolts being used each end. The outside bars had clips to connect them across the gap just at the end of the crosshead stroke – the slidebars acquired the name of 'rabbits' ears' in some quarters. The crossheads themselves were steel castings with gunmetal strips inserted in the top and bottom bearing surfaces which, should the whitemetal bearing surfaces have over-heated and run, would prevent the steel casting from scoring the slide bars. The gudgeon pins had cast-iron slit washers at the outer end and were retained by nuts and cotters. Unlike the GWR, the LMS used cast-iron packings for the piston rod stuffing boxes and Stanier did not insist on a change to the rope packing to which he had been accustomed. The crank axle of the leading coupled wheels was of a built-up type, the webs being a carbon steel (0.4 to 0.45 percent carbon content) and the remainder steel with a carbon content of 0.3 to 0.35 per cent.

The new coupled wheel diameter on the tread was 6ft 6in, unlike the Royal Scot class which had 6ft 9in wheels. The obvious influence was the GWR King class with that size of driving wheels, but in the published descriptions of the time, based on official handouts it is stated that the smaller size was considered very desirable in order to obtain maximum power combined with a free-running engine – this objective was indeed achieved, even though this small reduction was regarded as a break with convention. The coupled wheel centres were steel castings, the same pattern being used for all these wheels. They had rims of triangular section, not only having ample strength, but were considered by some commentators to be of pleasing appearance. A departure from previous LMS practice was the increase in width of these wheels by $\frac{1}{4}$in to $5\frac{3}{4}$in. Balance weights were added in a simple manner by attaching two steel plates, one either side of the spokes, and adding the appropriate amount of lead filling as dictated by the wheel balancing process. All tyres had Gibson ring fixing, with a retaining ring. The coupled wheel tyres were

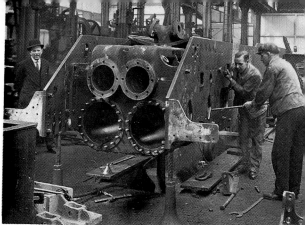

(*top*) Frames of No 6200 showing inside cylinder casting in position. *LMS.*

(*above*) View looking towards back of inside cylinders through motion bracket. *LMS.*

(*left*) Composite view of the frames showing disposition of cylinders, stretchers, etc. *LMS, R. T. Ellis collection.*

open-hearth acid steel with a tensile strength of 50 to 55 tons/sq in, and the remainder were of a similar steel but having a tensile strength of 56 to 62 tons/sq in.

The distance between the main frames was 4ft 1¼in and their thickness 1¼in. In thinking out the design of the frames the usual LMS practice of adding internal horizontal cross stretchers was questioned, and it was decided that by using heavier plates less staying of the frames was needed, so making them somewhat more flexible than before. In addition to the two vertical stretchers that were placed close to the intermediate and trailing coupled wheels, cross stays were used to prevent the frames from closing in at the bottom, a trouble experienced beforehand with large-boilered locomotives. It was at the trailing end below the firebox that an entirely new arrangement was designed, but in fact it was virtually the sole design feature of the ill-fated Fowler Pacific that was carried onto the Stanier locomotives. There were two separate hind-end frame plates for each side and they were 'spliced' to the main frame, the outer one being splayed outwards. Both had an upward sweep to clear the trailing truck and were attached to the rear buffer beam. The inner plates were 1¼in thick and were set slightly inwards to carry the centre casting for the truck; they also carried the rear dragbox. The outer plates were 1in thick.

The design of the frames introduced an obvious weak point at the joint of the main plates and the rear extension below the firebox. The frames were most vulnerable at this point when being lifted, so all rivets at the joint were a turned driving fit and riveted cold, welding being added at all the outside edges. The boiler was carried not only by the two smokebox saddles already described but two intermediate supports on top of the frames, the first just to the rear of the smokebox tubeplate, the other between the intermediate and trailing coupled wheels, and at the firebox. These supports had gunmetal bearing strips to allow for boiler expansion, and side clips as well. At the leading end of the firebox the base of the foundation ring formed another bearer, having a gunmetal strip affixed which rested on bearer brackets on the frame. At the other end of the firebox a 'diaphragm' plate was attached to the foundation ring at the mid-point which was attached at its lower edge to the dragbox; the 'diaphragm' plate was approximately vertical and had to have sufficient play to allow for the rearward movement of the boiler when in steam.

The springs of the coupled wheels were made up of laminated silico-manganese steel plates held together by a steel buckle, and they were attached to the axlebox by a heavy link, a large diameter pin passing through it and lugs under the axlebox. The outer ends of the springs were held by spring links resting on pads with gunmetal bearing surfaces and spherical steel washers to allow for relative movement. The spring links had screwed ends for nuts which allowed adjustment of the loads on individual springs; when the load was correct the nuts were retained by driven pins. The other end of the spring links had a head and between them and each spring bracket (which was attached to the frame) damper springs were fitted. These consisted of alternate thin steel plates and rubber pads. When the technical description was released to the public it was stated that one of the locomotives would have compensated coupled wheels spring gear, but that never happened.

The locomotive brake was operated by a steam cylinder ahead of the firebox – through the rigging it applied the brake blocks to the front of each coupled wheel. These blocks were carried on hangers, suspended from brackets attached to the frame. The total weight on the rails ranking for adhesion was 67½ tons, the braked proportion being 74 percent, or 47.8 percent of the total locomotive weight. No braking was applied to the bogie or the trailing truck, the LMS having decided a few years earlier to do away with bogie brakes, partly on fears of their causing derailments — it seems to have escaped the notice of locomotive engineers that electric multiple-units (or for that matter a motor train when running with a coach in the lead) had braked bogies at the front!

Stanier introduced a new form of axlebox to the LMS, based on Swindon practice, and this feature perhaps more than any other made life on a day-to-day basis in running sheds just that little bit less hectic (not to say frustrating at times) by reducing significantly the incidence of 'hot boxes', an ailment that afflicted so many LMS engines, particularly those of Derby design. By providing a far more generous bearing surface and excellent lubrication the fear of overheating was virtually non-existent on the Stanier classes, a factor which enhanced their availability for work, as a stoppage for a difficult repair job was avoided. Equally enginemen no longer had a fear of running hot on a journey. For the Pacifics the coupled axle bearings were 10in long on an axle 10in in diameter. The axlebox itself was a steel casting fitted with pressed-in brasses having white-metal crowns. Great care was taken in the assembly and fitting of axleboxes which was part of the secret, but equally as important was the lubrication, achieved by feeding the lubricating oil to the crown from where it spread through shallow feeding channels over the axle bearing face. This oil was fed under pressure from the mechanical lubricator on the right-hand side of the frame, it having ten feeds. Connecting pipes to each axlebox included a back-pressure valve (on the axlebox) and a flexible rubber hose to accommodate relative movement between the frames and axleboxes. The mechanical

lubricators were driven by links connected to the outside valve gear and for axleboxes the minimum rate of supply was 2oz per 100 miles of running; however, by altering the links the oil supply could be increased if desired. In addition to the lubrication provided at the top of each bearing, axleboxes had deep oil wells in underkeeps which applied oil below the journal by means of pads fitted on a light sprung frame. The pad was a mixture of horsehair and wool and included worsted feeders which drew up the oil from the reservoir. These underkeeps were removable, except on crank axles, for cleaning, pad inspection and refilling.

The leading bogie was of a type entirely new to the LMS and greatly superior to previous forms, being a copy of that used by the GWR and derived originally from the De Glehn compound Atlantics obtained by the Great Western Railway in 1903–5, so much so that at Crewe Works they were called 'French bogies'. The essential feature was the use of side bolsters to transmit the load from the main frames to the bogie and so great was the improvement in riding that higher speeds, even if not intended, through curves and crossings did not constitute a danger. In two well-known incidents to be mentioned it is certain that derailment would have followed the passage of curves if this type of bogie had not existed. The bogie had bar frames, a weight-reducing choice,

Details at the trailing end, showing the exhaust steam injector, rear frame extension and side doors of the ashpan. *The Railway Gazette*.

with a centre casting which engaged the locomotive bogie pin, a maximum lateral travel of $2\frac{7}{8}$in either way being catered for, there being stop brackets on the frame to prevent further movement because of the limited clearance between the bogie wheels and the inside cylinders. The bearing springs were similar to the coupled wheel springs, other than being inverted and axleboxes were generally similar to the coupled wheel axleboxes, except that only underkeep lubrication was provided and that the boxes were solid gunmetal. The side bearers each consisted of a sliding cup resting on the bogie bracket bearing surfaces well lubricated. Side control was provided by flexible check springs, their initial loading being two tons and three tons when the bogie moved across by its full travel. The bogie was identical each end so that it could be turned round, only the guard irons having to be moved from one end to the other.

At the rear of the locomotive support was provided by a Bissel truck, its arm being anchored 6ft 10in ahead of the axle centre line to a stretcher immediately in front of the firebox throatplate. Locomotive weight was transmitted by side bolsters similar to those on the bogie, but they had to be inside the truck frames. As on the bogie the axleboxes were solid gunmetal with white metal crowns and the laminated springs were placed above them, having adjustable screwed links and rubber damper springs. The journals were 12in long on axles of 7½in diameter, being lubricated by oil pads in the underkeeps, access being gained by removing external cover plates. Lateral travel of 4¼in each way was allowed and flexible check springs were fitted, their initial loading being 1·44 tons, the maximum centring force being 2·96 tons. The design of this truck was very successful in ensuring smooth riding.

Between the locomotive and tender the intermediate drawgear was controlled by a laminated spring housed in the tender dragbox. Its initial load was six tons and the main drawbar was directly connected to the spring buckle. At the other end of the drawbar the main drawbar pin fitted with a clearance limited to no more than ¹⁄₁₆in in the drawbar's hole, the intention being the elimination of lateral movement between the locomotive and tender. The drawbar was further held in tension by the action of the side buffers housed in the tender frame, which being spring-loaded forced the locomotive apart from the tender by acting on case-hardened pads rivetted to the engine buffer beam. The pads had inclined faces.

The locomotive hammer-blow, calculated at five revolutions per second, was

Each pair of coupled wheels – 0·14 ton,
Total for locomotive – 0·42 ton.

To balance the revolving weight of the big-end journals in the crank axle webs it was necessary to extend the opposite end of each web.

Stanier's hallmark on the LMS was taper boilers and they set a new standard of maintenance and economy, rather more advantageous to the workshops but giving less trouble in daily service than existing LMS types, although the large Derby-style Belpaire boilers were little trouble. Stanier's initial failing with his boilers was in the extent of superheating applied. He was used to small superheaters which did little more than dry the steam, but they had been successful on the GWR since introduction because they avoided lubrication troubles which had been encountered elsewhere and rather set back the progress of superheating in some quarters. The fault at Swindon lay in not realising that even by 1930 lubricating oils had become

available which allowed a greater degree of superheat. Some years later, in 1941, Stanier admitted that he had not seen that with the larger diameter elements used by the LMS a centre core of steam as it passed through the elements did not get effective additional heat and therefore steam passing to the cylinders still contained a large proportion of saturated steam. Even with the hard water problems afflicting so much of the LMS in England, Stanier boilers gave a better life than others — a boiler could be expected to last up to 18–20 years before requiring a new firebox followed by a further 15 years or so before condemnation, when plates were wasting away to scrapping size. It so happened that British Railways was well into the replacement of steam when the time came to produce the first replacement boilers, so apart from a very small number of spares built up to 1960 there was never a programme of renewals for longer life Stanier classes. For the Pacifics this was unlikely to have happened as the expected locomotive life was much the same as that for the boilers, and their replacement was due in any case when the diesels and electrics arrived.

The boiler barrel tapered uniformly from the throatplate to the smokebox tubeplate, the internal diameters being 6ft 3in and 5ft 8⅝in respectively. The distance between tubeplates was no less than 20ft 9in. The tube arrangement comprised of 16 steel superheater tubes of 5⅛in and 170 steel boiler tubes of 2¼in (both figures outside diameters). The superheater, or flue tubes were specially thickened at the firebox tubeplate and screwed at 11 threads per inch, a practice new to the LMS; when fitted they were first expanded on the water side and then beaded over. The small boiler tubes were simply beaded over after expansion. Ample water circulating space was allowed between the outermost tubes and the barrel plates. Welding was applied to the boiler barrel longitudinal seams for a distance of 1ft 0in at each end, being butt-jointed with cover strips of ¾in thick inside and out. The barrel had three rings, telescopically jointed; these circumferential joints were double rivetted. The individual rings had plates of ¹³⁄₁₆in at the front, ²⁷⁄₃₂in in the middle and ⅞in at the rear, their respective lengths being 7ft 2½in, 7ft 7in and 6ft 1¾in. The smokebox tubeplate, recessed 7⅛in into the barrel, was ¹³⁄₁₆in thick and flanged to drumhead form. In a drawing published in *The Locomotive Magazine*, together with a detailed

:scription, it can be worked out that the outside :ameter of the tubeplate was 5ft 8⅝in not 5ft 9in published. The throatplate was a saddle, ⅞in ick, unlike narrow firebox boilers which had a roatplate which formed a ring into which the rrel fitted. The barrel was attached to the ebox by a short parallel ring of ⅞in plate and ıtside diameter 6ft 4¾in. The outer firebox rapper was made up of three ⅝in plates, butt-inted at about water level, with corner plates on oth sides forming the shoulders of the firebox. he firebox backplate sloped from the undation ring, except in the upper part which as vertical, being flanged to form the firedoor oening. To give the boiler longitudinal strength ıere were six 1¾in diameter stays extending for ıe full length, two from the tubeplate to brackets ı the second ring and another two from the beplate to the third ring, while at the other end ıere were two stays from the firebox backplate to ıe top corners of the firebox and four extending the third ring of the barrel. Across the top of ıe firebox there were no fewer than 42 stays. All ıe boiler plates were made of 2% nickel steel.

The foundation ring was a forging 3¾in wide ıd 4in deep, attached to both the outer steel rebox plates and the copper inner firebox plates y double rivetting. The copper firebox ımprised of plates ⅝in thick with a 1in thick

tubeplate. It was stayed at the sides by ⅞in copper stays apart from the fire area where ⅝in mild steel stays were used, except the two outer vertical rows at each end where copper was used. Both the copper and steel stays were reduced in diameter in the section between the plates and were rivetted over at both ends, except that the steel stays had nuts on the fire ends (to facilite renewal when wasting away). The seams of the copper firebox were single-rivetted. Certain of the stays, those used at the curved portion of the throatplate where it formed a combustion chamber and all the outside rows, were a copper-nickel alloy (80/20 proportion). The firehole was flanged and oval in shape, having a thickening plate around the lower lip to protect the joint; the aperture was 1ft 7in wide and 1ft 2in deep. The distance between the firebox crown and the outer shell was 2ft 0in so giving ample steam space above the water level. The steam collector, placed just ahead of the firebox as high as possible, presented a long narrow orifice to the entering steam which was then conveyed through a 7in diameter main steampipe to the regulator and superheater header. The regulator was a distinct departure from LMS practice, being

Boiler being lowered into position on 20 June 1933. *The Railway Gazette.*

Partially completed boiler for Princess Royal Class, with its copper firebox alongside. The next stage was to fit the latter and then drill both wrapper plates and copper box for stays. *The Railway Gazette*.

incorporated into the superheater header. It was operated by a conventional rod passing right through from the firebox backplate into the back of the header and was lubricated by means of a small sight feed lubricator in the cab which could be set by the driver; about one drop of cylinder oil per five minutes was sufficient, but to assist in moving the regulator a balance weight was added to the regulator handle.

The firebox had a grate area of 45 sq ft, regarded as large enough to afford a low rate of combustion and ensure that on long runs the firebars would not become unduly clinkered. At the front end the firebox was 7ft 1in across the foundation ring, tapering to 6ft 1in at the footplate end, its shape being intended to assist hand firing in the back corners. The water legs were 3¾in wide at the foundation ring, gradually widening to 5½in at the top of the firebox, an important means of improving water circulation.

Normal LMS firedoors were fitted, opened by a single lever on the driver's side – its position was a curious relic of the earliest days of steam engines when it was usual for the driver to open the firedoor while the fireman fed the fire, a practice retained in Ireland to the end of steam, but long since given up in Britain. In the firehole there was

a loose cast-iron ring in the lower part whic[h] protected the plates, and a steel baffle placed i[n] the upper section. The latter was easil[y] removable and was shaped to deflect secondar[y] air entering through the firehole onto the surfac[e] of the fire. On the left-hand side a scree[n] projected to protect the driver from the glare [of] the fire. The grate had cast-iron firebars in thre[e] sections, but no drop or rocking grate wa[s] provided. The first section of the grate, below th[e] firedoor, was level, being 2ft 11½in long, th[e] remainder being sloped.

Many of the boiler mountings were of standar[d] LMS type, including the safety-valves, wate[r] gauge frames and protectors. The four Ross po[p] safety-valves, mounted on top of the firebox[,] were set at 250lb/sq in and were identical wit[h] those used on the Royal Scot class. A benefici[al] change from LMS practice was the fitting of [a] steam manifold on top of the firebox, just withi[n] the cab and below the roof. Having a stea[m] supply shut-off valve, the manifold had stea[m] control valves for injectors, ejector, locomotiv[e] and tender steam brake supply, carriage warmin[g] supply, ashpan flush injector, regulator sight fee[d] lubricator and whistle. The whistle la[y] horizontally above the firebox just in front of th[e] cab. Its operating lever had a handle on each si[de] of the footplate, rather short in fact and not s[o] easy for some drivers to reach.

Other cab controls were the blower handl[e]

which was placed on the firedoor plate so that it could be reached easily by either of the enginemen, injector controls on the fireman's side for the Davies & Metcalf exhaust steam injector and on the driver's side for the Gresham & Craven live steam injector. The boiler feedwater was delivered into the barrel through clacks in a top-feed casting mounted on the barrel where usually there would be a dome; at first sight it appeared that the boiler had a dome, but although so shaped, the cover housed no more than the top feed. Below the clacks inside the barrel the feed was delivered through nozzles onto removable trays (for cleaning) where it was first heated and then mingled with the boiler contents, so reducing the shock effect of the entry of cold water; the trays were in effect a very simple form of pre-heater.

Although the locomotive and tender were steam-braked, the brake control for fitted trains was vacuum, so an ejector had to be provided. Previously LMS standard classes had a Dreadnought-type ejector, mounted at the front of the boiler on the left-side. On the 'Lizzies' the ejector was situated on the side of the firebox just ahead of the cab on the left-hand side, having a waste pipe which ran alongside the boiler barrel below the handrail to discharge into the smokebox below the chimney, and a connection to the vacuum brake pipe which ran from front to rear mostly below the left-side platform. The driver's brake valve was of type new to the LMS, being a modified version of that marketed by Gresham & Craven — this had three positions, 'running', 'brake on' and 'ejector on'. Because of the crosshead-driven vacuum pump it was necessary to use the ejector only to release the brake or when running at low speed.

The boiler, firebox and cylinders were covered with plastic magnesia to reduce radiated heat losses. When applying this to the first boiler it seemed impossible to get the substance to stick, although it was known that it had to be applied to a heated boiler – it was discovered at the inspiration of Mr Robin Riddles that it was best applied by throwing it hard at the boiler! The outer clothing comprised sheet steel (14 swg), supported on steel framework (known as 'crinolines' in the shops), the joints being covered by steel bands.

Special thought had to be given to the design of the ashpan because of space limitations imposed by the layout of the trailing ends of the frames.

Footplate layout of the Princess Royal Class. *LMS.*

The ashpan plates were copper-bearing steel. There were three damper doors, a front one facing forward and a middle and a rear, both the latter facing backwards. In addition there were side damper doors placed between the bottom of the foundation ring and the top of the ashpan sides. At this point the bottom of the ashpan was very close to the firebars and it was to provide sufficient primary air to the grate that the side doors were fitted. There were separate control handles for the front middle and rear doors, and a handle for the side doors. The type of lever provided to control damper doors on LMS locomotives was somewhat archaic and not at a particularly good design, depending on crude slots in the simple lifting handles to hold doors in the required positions. A refinement of doubtful value was the provision of a flushing pipe inside the ashpan, intended to assist in keeping it clean, drawing a steam supply through a small Gresham & Craven vertical type injector and its water from the exhaust steam injector.

Derby had stuck to what was becoming an old-fashioned design of smokebox for LMS standard locomotives; in particular its door was not always airtight. Stanier introduced a more reliable and airtight type usually referred to as a 'drumhead smokebox'. Its diameter was 6ft 1in internally, the copper bearing steel plates being ½in thick, and it was attached to the barrel for its full circumference by a 2³⁄₁₆in steel ring. Inside the smokebox the two live steampipes passed round the sides to sharp elbows, from which the branches to the outside cylinders passed outside the smokebox and then backwards to a further bend leading down into the steamchest. The connection to the inside steamchest was through a further elbow on the inside cylinder casting. The four exhaust pipes combined at a saddle casting towards the rear of the smokebox and discharged through a single 5¹¹⁄₁₆in diameter blastpipe which had a novelty for the LMS. This was a Swindon-style jumper top, designed to lift due to higher back-pressure when working hard and form an enlarged blastpipe orifice such that back-pressure would then reduce and hopefully

lead to a reduction in coal consumption. Across the back of the smokebox, spark deflector plates diverted tube gases downwards below the top of the blastpipe. At the throat of the chimney there was a circular casting which formed both a silencer for the vacuum ejector waste and a blower ring, the latter having its steam supply controlled from the footplate. At the base of the blastpipe there was a branch pipe which took exhaust steam through a large diameter pipe, which included a centrifugal dirt collector situated between the leading and driving coupled wheels, the pipe itself remaining above the axles and then passing outside the frames ahead of the trailing coupled wheels to pass just below the platform alongside the firebox before dropping down to the exhaust steam injector.

Externally the rim of the chimney stood 1ft 0in above the smokebox into which it extended internally. It had an internal diameter of 1ft 4¼in at the blower ring casting, the joint being 1ft 8⁹⁄₁₆in below the top of the chimney. Below the blower ring the petticoat extended a further 11¾in downwards, having widened to 2ft 2¾in.

The smokebox door was of a type new to the LMS, being retained by a dart and centre bar instead of securing lugs around its circumference. Airtightness was obtained by machining the faces of both the flanged front ring of the smokebox and the dished door to form bevelled 45 degree mating surfaces. The door swung on a pair of hinged straps. The upper lamp bracket was fixed to the top of the door, which also had a handrail across the upper part and carried a cast numberplate.

Another distinctive feature of Stanier locomotives was the cab, which had large side windows and an extended roof. Overall the width was 8ft 10in. In the process of determining the ideal layout of the controls a wooden model was built so that positions could be varied before the location of any individual control was finally agreed. Of the two windows each side the rear one could be moved forward behind the front one to give a full opening and indeed always seemed to be in that position. On the left, the driver's side, there was an external small glass screen on a pivotted frame; it could lie flat against the cabside or be turned outwards to act as a draught deflector for forward lookout. On both sides at the front of the cab there were hinged windows. Across the front of the cab above the firebox there was a series of ½in diameter holes so that a

The front end of No 6200 as completed. *LMS*.

urrent of air would pass along the inside of the oof and extra ventilation was provided by a liding hatch in the roof. Tip-up seats were fitted n each side of the footplate. Gangway doors, prung to keep them closed, filled the gap etween locomotive and tender; these folding oors had rubber extensions at the bottom to help ll the gap, and were retained by a pivotted bar vhich dropped into a catch on the door furthest way from the wingplate. Behind the seats the absides were turned inwards as wingplates to ive some measure of draught exclusion and add trength to the cab structure.

Apart from the controls noted on the boiler, here was the reversing screw on the left-hand ide, ashpan damper door levers and pet-cock for he slacking pipe (used for spraying the coal and ashing-down the footplate). The floor was made p with wooden planks. One tunnel in particular, he single bore at Linslade on the down main, was close fit round the Pacifics and more than once n entering at high speed the ensuing draught lasted away the footboards so leaving both men o make the best of standing on the dragbox! "here were no steps on the locomotive at the railing end because of the throw-over of the xtended frames, and the adjacent steps on the ender had to be used.

Stanier decided that mechanical sanding was uite sufficient, although it must have been :nown to somebody in the Derby drawing office hat in October–November 1926 the GWR Castle ad shown that it was quite ineffective in exposed laces like Shap. Sand was contained in abricated steel hoppers with extension pipes to nake filling an easier job. Feed pipes applied and in front of the leading intermediate coupled vheels and to the rear of the latter as well. When he sanding lever was pushed to apply sand when oing forward a jet of hot water was directed onto he rails to wash away the sand after the wheels ad passed over it, the object being the revention of interference with signalling track ircuits. The water de-sanding valve was fitted on he left side of the firebox.

As built, there was no steam heating onnection at the front of the locomotive, only a upply through a tender hose being provided. team was taken from the manifold through a educing valve set at 50lb/sq in.

In addition to the mechanical lubrication lready mentioned there were various grease oints on the locomotive for details such as Bissel

truck anchor pin, top and bottom brake hanger pins, reversing gear and intermediate side buffer heads.

An unexpected departure from Derby practice was the choice of a Caledonian Railway type of hooter for the whistle. Just who decided upon this choice or influenced Stanier seems to have escaped recording, but it should be remembered that after a 'whistle concert' at Horwich in late December 1923 the Caledonian hooter had been selected to be the standard type for the LMS, only to be quashed summarily by the Motive Power Officer who insisted on the Midland whistle. It could well have been H.P.M. Beames, formerly Chief Mechanical Engineer of the LNWR and a participant in the 1923 decision who, no doubt with great delight at scoring one off Derby, drew Stanier's attention to the hooter. The result was a sound that distinguished, at least south of the border, a Stanier locomotive unseen or when heard at night.

Diagrams for the Princess Royal Class always quoted locomotive weights of 21 tons on the bogies, 22 tons 10 cwt on each coupled axle and 16 tons on the truck, a total of 104 tons 10 cwt. The first diagram gave this as the estimated weight, succeeding diagrams gave it as the weight in working order. An apparently official total weight of 103 tons 15 cwt has also been given, but in reality they must have been as much as six or seven tons heavier. Indeed, it has been stated that No 6200 turned the scales at 111 tons when first weighed, so that some attempt was made to reduce weight on No 6201 by enlarging 'lightening holes' and thinning down castings. Whatever the form of the locomotive no variation in weight was ever quoted officially.

Tenders are described in Chapter 7 and the developments which followed the introduction of the first two 'Lizzies', together with the construction of ten more in 1935 follow in Chapter 5.

It is interesting to find in contemporary issues of The Railway Gazette a strong criticism from an obviously knowledgeable correspondent, comparing the new design with the Royal Scot Class which the writer claimed (rightly so it proved) had 50 degrees Fahrenheit higher superheat. The writer further considered that a combustion chamber was essential — he suggested 3ft 0in — and that there should be 32 elements at least. That he was so prophetic will be seen in Chapter 5.

CHAPTER 4

THE 'TURBOMOTIVE'

The first signs of interest by the LMS in turbine propulsion for a steam locomotive appeared a little after the first three Pacifics had been authorised in July 1932. Then in February 1933 an expenditure of £6,000 for the machinery was authorised and work went ahead which resulted in one of the most successful experimental locomotives ever to run in Great Britain.

There had been four previous attempts in Great Britain to produce a turbine-driven steam locomotive, the Reid–Ramsey turbo-electric of 1910 built by the North British Locomotive Company and tried on the North Eastern Railway; the Reid–Macleod turbine condensing locomotive of 1924 which utilised parts of the aforementioned machine and ran trials on the LMS in Scotland; a contemporary Armstrong–Whitworth turbo-electric built for the Ramsey Company of Newcastle-upon-Tyne which ran briefly on trial on the Lancashire & Yorkshire Railway section of the LMS in 1923; and the Beyer-Ljungström 2,000hp turbo-electric locomotive of 1926 which ran for some months between St Pancras and Manchester on the Midland Division of the LMS. All of these projects were privately financed and the trials over the railway companies' tracks undertaken with a measure of benevolent tolerance by operating staff. With the LMS experiment it was the company's property that was on trial. It had a far better chance when things went wrong, as there was always somebody superior who could ensure that testing was resumed following any unhappy interference with day-to-day operating; in fact a major difference between the LMS locomotive and the others was that it worked with very little specialist supervision, running almost like a conventional locomotive, drivers and firemen working it within their normal link turns of duty.

In 1932 a quite different approach to the use of a turbine drive was showing considerable promise on the Grangesberg-Oxelosund Railway in Sweden and compared well with otherwise similar reciprocating engines of the same type. The important change compared with earlier attempts was the absence of a condenser, a feature so closely associated with turbines that no one before had the temerity not to include one! Condenser performance and maintenance problems had been a major stumbling block beforehand, their size also adding considerably to

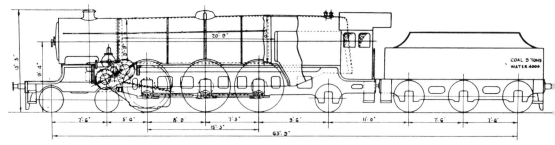

PROPOSED 2600 H.P. TURBINE LOCOMOTIVE SYSTEM LJUNGSTRÖM.

DIAMETER OF DRIVERS...6'-9"	GRATE AREA .... 45 SQ F.	TRACTIVE EFFORT MAX...20·4 MET TONS
STEAM PRESSURE ____ 250 LBS	HEATING SURFACE TOTAL...2100 SQ F.	MAX SPEED .... 90 MILES P.H.
	WEIGHT ON DRIVERS ..... 68 MET TONS	

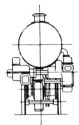

Fig 8 Proposed turbine locomotive, 1933. *By Permission of the Institution of Mechanical Engineers, Journal 191, Paper No 458.*

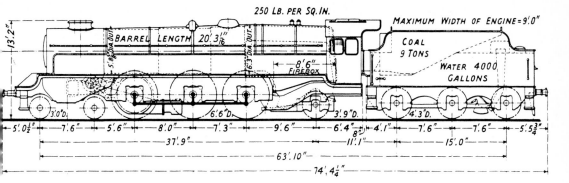

Fig 9 Stanier 4–6–2 turbine passenger locomotive. *The Railway Gazette.*

he length and weight of experimental machines. On the Swedish locomotive the turbine was mounted on extended frames in front of the smokebox and drove through a triple-reduction gear and jackshaft. The extra length at the front end did not become a problem with turntables and other locations because because reduced water consumption allowed the use of a four-wheel tender instead of the usual six-wheel type, so keeping in line with the wheelbases of the conventional locomotives then in use. It has been stated that the performance of this turbine locomotive was successful enough to build a further three.

It was Dr Guy of Metropolitan–Vickers who took the initiative and interested Stanier in the Swedish experiment. Both visited that country in the autumn of 1932 – they were accompanied by the chief draughtsman from Derby and an assistant from Metropolitan–Vickers. They formed a very favourable impression of the locomotive's performance and after assessment of the possibilities expressed the opinion that the construction of a turbine-drive machine in Great Britain was justified. Despite the hardship of the times, the LMS board took the brave step of allowing the project to go forward, not begrudging the risk of abortive expenditure when most of their efforts had to be directed to achieving widespread economies throughout the company. There was the closest of co-operation between Derby and the turbine manufacturers, but apart from the transmission as much as possible was standard with the conventional members of the class, although the layout of the footplate, smokebox and draughting had to differ. There was one other feature unique to this locomotive at the time, the use of Timken roller-bearing axleboxes throughout, although at the early stages of design there were worries that weight limitations might have prevented their use

on the coupled axles. Due to the absence of reciprocating parts it was possible to exceed the normally permitted axle loading maximum of 22½ tons, two of the coupled axles being laden to more than 23 tons.

The advantages sought by experimenting with turbine propulsion were:

1. A lower factor of adhesion, due partly to the purely rotary transmission, permitting a higher starting tractive effort with the same weight on coupled wheels.
2. Drawbar pull and tractive effort for any power output constant throughout each revolution.
3. Absence of reciprocating parts, allowing moving parts to be balanced — therefore hammer-blow would not exist.
4. Elimination of wear and tear of reciprocating parts and reduction of associated friction losses leading to a 6–8% advantage in mechanical efficiency.
5. Elimination of valves and pistons which would reduce time out of service for routine examinations.
6. Expansion of steam in the turbine from boiler pressure to back pressure rather than exhausting at some 50lb/sq in higher would lead to fuel economy.

Because there were no problems of lubrication for valves and pistons, steam temperatures could be as much as 150°F higher, further enhancing fuel economy by some 6%, but in practice it had to be accepted that such a saving was unlikely to be better than 3% in a non-condensing system as it was not possible to exhaust so close to back pressure as in a fully condensing plant.

The specification of the LMS locomotive required that it should be capable of working

No 6202 after the fitting of its second boiler having a dome and enlarged superheater. The 'Turbomotive' stands here at Shrewsbury. *Real Photographs/Ian Allan.*

trains of 500 tons between Euston and Glasgow, needing a turbine of 2,600hp, giving an estimated starting tractive effort of 40,000lb, or 12,000lb sustained at 70mph, the speed at which the turbine reached its maximum efficiency. After consideration of a variety of proposals it was decided that the locomotive should conform as closely as possible to the other two Pacifics and this led to triple-reduction gearing and a higher turbine speed than initially planned. Many have praised the appearance of No 6202 and it was often claimed to be the most outstanding aesthetically of British steam classes. Readers no doubt have their thoughts on that matter.

There were two turbines, one for forward running, the other for reverse. The forward turbine was on the left-hand side of the locomotive, housed in the bulbous casing below platform level and the front end of the full length covering, and occupying much the same position as the outside cylinder would have done. It had 16 stages, designed to maintain a high efficiency over the speed range 35mph to 90mph which was the maximum permitted for this locomotive; the peak efficiency occurred at 62mph (7,060 revolutions per minute) which was ideal for express train running at the time. At that speed No 6202 was capable of some 600hp more at the rail than the rest of the 'Lizzies'. The boiler had a standard regulator which was fully opened during running. Superheated steam passed

through a strainer situated outside the smokebox above the turbine and was admitted to the turbine through a control box having six valves for forward running and three for reverse, operated by hand from the footplate, the linkage passing alongside the boiler within the large left side casing. The valves were opened quickly in succession, the number open determining the power produced by the turbines. The forward turbine was permanently coupled to the leading axle through double helical triple reduction gearing, the ratio being 34·4:1, so that at 90mph the turbine speed was 13,500 revolutions per minute. This axle, in order to allow free movement because of the rise and fall of its axleboxes, had a pair of solid forged arms which were attached to the final drive gear wheel by means of a yoke and pivotted links. The gear wheel itself comprised of a gear rim and two wheel centres running on white metal bearings fixed to the gear case enclosing the whole train – it had been necessary to use such bearings because no way had been found in which roller bearings could be used. Power was transmitted through a series of laminated springs arranged circumferentially around the wheel, so relieving the teeth from shocks incurred through direct contact. The high-speed pinion was connected to the turbine shaft by a hollow quill shaft and two diaphragm couplings to ensure sufficient flexibility. The first reduction gears were given limited transverse play upon their spindles so that there was an even load distribution along their teeth. The final drive unit lay along the longitudinal centre line of the locomotive and remained connected to the forward turbine at all times so that when running in reverse that turbine was freely rotating; steam was then bled from the reverse turbine to fill the forward turbine casing in order to provide adequate cooling.

The low-power reverse turbine, mounted on the right-hand side of the locomotive drove the gear train by a further single-reduction gear, having a ratio of 77:1, but it was de-meshed during forward running. It was smaller and designed only for light running or station movements. Steam was fed through three valves, opened to the number required, contained in the same control box as the forward valves. The additional reduction gear was carried on the same axis as the first pinion of the main transmission, and was engaged to the main transmission by a splined sliding shaft and a dog-clutch, operated from the footplate. As installed the clutch was manoeuvred by a small steam motor which proved to be rather troublesome and an unnecessary complication, so it was replaced by a manual gear which proved to be entirely satisfactory. To overcome 'tooth-on-tooth' conditions which would prevent engagement, a ratchet inching device was fitted.

In the place of the conventional reversing screw the driver had a main control box in front of him. Its solitary handle controlled the turbine steam admission valves, being turned clockwise for the forward turbine and anti-clockwise for the reverse turbine. An interlocking device had to be fitted, after a major failure, which prevented engagement of the reverse turbine clutch unless the control handle was in the neutral position (vertical) and all steam valves closed. The reverse turbine valve could not be opened until the clutch was correctly engaged, nor could the forward valves be opened if the reverse turbine was in gear. As further protection the handle to operate the clutch could not be moved until the locomotive was stationary.

Although the turbine lubrication system was a source of major failures it was a primary factor in the success of the system! The turbine units were completely enclosed, turbine and pinion bearings and gears being lubricated by a force-fed system using three pumps. The bearings were fed under pressure while the gear teeth received oil from sprayers. The reversible primary oil pump, driven by the main slow-speed wheel through another gear wheel, was situated in the oil well to

the rear of the leading coupled axle and pressurised the system only when the locomotive was in motion. There was also a steam-driven reciprocating pump, situated on the left-hand side of the locomotive, which was necessary to supplement the primary pump and to pressurise the system on starting and during slow running. It was laid down that this pump was to be kept going at all times and for up to 30 minutes after completing a journey in order to pass oil through both the turbine shafts to cool their bearings. Oil from both the gear-driven pump and the reciprocating pump passed into an air-cooler type radiator, protected by non-return valves. The radiator was placed between the frames at the front of the locomotive in the position that the inside cylinder valve chests would have occupied. Illustrations of No 6202 show that when running the cover plate below the smokebox was raised and held open, drivers being specially instructed to open it before starting to ensure a proper air supply. On the footplate a pair of gauges registered the oil temperature at the inlet and outlet of the cooler, the inlet varying from 120°F to 180°F, the outlet being some 40°F cooler.

From the cooler oil passed to four areas, feeding the forward turbine bearings, the high-speed pinion bearings and sprayer, the intermediate and slow-speed pinion bearings and sprayer and the reverse turbine. A gauge on the footplate indicated the oil pressure which increased to about 16lb/sq in at 60mph and remained at 7lb/sq in when only the steam pump was working. The feed to the reverse turbine passed through an automatic plunger which during forward running allowed only a small flow of oil to pass, but in reverse it was fully opened. The major modification to the lubricating oil system was the provision of a second reciprocating steam pump supplying the reverse turbine, following three major failures of that component. This pump drew oil from the sump through a non-return valve and a strainer and then passed it directly to the reverse turbine, having a separate gauge on the footplate which normally indicated about 7lb/sq in. This pump was also run continuously.

In the oil sump there was an Auto-Klean strainer with magnetic inserts, which was checked and cleaned daily. The turbine gland ejectors could not entirely prevent steam ingress into the lubricating oil and in practice it was found that about one gallon of water was drained from the sump each day. The oil had to be changed after 6,000 miles of running. There were two pressure relief valves in the system, one in the sump for the gear-driven pump, the other in the second supply to the reverse turbine.

With any experimental locomotive failure has to be regarded as a possibility, often causing expensive repairs or modification. The turbine drive of No 6202 was no exception, but compared with many other unconventional steam locomotives the experiment was far more successful and longer lived — it was even continued with extreme difficulty through World War II, as it was necessary to use every locomotive that could turn a wheel, and in that respect its working passed out of a controlled experiment condition to that of normal daily use, a much more severe test of the system. Taking the first ten years, for which accurate information is freely available, there were 13 major failures, some leading to modification. Subsequent to 1945 there was not the opportunity to develop the project, but No 6202 continued to run intermittently until it was put aside after a failure which occurred at Rugby when working its usual job, the 8.30 a.m. down Liverpool, on Monday 21st November 1949. Afterwards the story of this locomotive took a different line (Chapter 5).

Of the thirteen major incidents, six were failures of the reverse turbine, oil leakage accounting for another four; there were two failures of the forward turbine and the other occurred in the flexible drive between the high-speed gear-wheel and the leading axle. Only one took place while working a passenger train, the others happening either when reversing or during shunting movements. These cases occurred as follows (mileage from new in brackets):

1. 8/1935 (6,100) Leakage of oil from turbine bearings.
2. 9/1935 (9,164) Failure of reversing mechanism.
3. 1/1936 (12,644) Failure of reverse turbine.
4. 5/1936 (40,653) Failure of reverse turbine.
5. 7/1936 (45,688) Leakage of oil from turbine bearings.
6. 1/1937 (78,812) Failure of forward turbine.
7. 11/1937 (125,791) Failure of reverse turbine.
8. 2/1939 (177,413) Failure of forward turbine.
9. 9/1941 (195,370) Failure of reverse turbine.
10. 11/1942 (219,243) Oil leakage from both turbines.
11. 7/1943 (249,261) Failure of flexible drive.
12. 12/1944 (252,473) Failure of reverse turbine bearing.
13. 4/1945 (270,233) Leakage of oil from turbine bearings.

The one failure with a passenger train was No 8 in the list above, occurring at Boxmoor.

The first failure of the reverse turbine was due to the clutch not engaging properly but nonetheless allowing the turbine to rotate when steam was applied. There was no interlock on the driver's control box to prevent opening of the steam valves without the proper engagement, and in this case the oil valve had not opened so that the bearing partially fused, the thrust bearing wearing badly and allowing the rotor to move laterally so that it rubbed against the stationary blades. There had been complaints that this turbine was not powerful enough so the opportunity was taken to redesign it and increase its power. At the same time the clutch and steam valves were modified so that they interlocked, the steam reversing cylinder was replaced by a hand screw on the control box, turbine thrust bearings were increased in area with improved lubrication and a visual indicator fitted so that clutch operation could be checked. The second failure, again in the reversing mechanism, occurred when steam leakage past the control valves caused the turbine to rotate immediately the clutch spindle left the inching gear. Stronger springs were fitted in the steam valves to ensure better seating and the method of reversing altered, it being required that the regulator must also be closed and the reverse turbine steamchest drain valve open during the operation. As a direct result of this incident a new clutch shaft and inching gear were fitted, designed to make reversing more foolproof by using the ratchet to hold positively the shaft until the teeth had begun to engage.

On four occasions the reverse turbine failed due to lack of lubrication of the bearings and lateral movement of the rotor. To overcome this the width of the pinion bearings was increased, the oil supply passages enlarged and the automatic valve altered to give more lubrication when the turbine was not engaged. However, two failures occurred subsequently with similar results, and it was after the September 1941 incident that the second reciprocating steam pump was fitted as it was clear that extra grooves which had been made in the turbine bearings and the pipework modified so that all the lubricating oil passed through the air-cooler were not a palliative. These changes were completely successful and eliminated the reverse turbine as a source of failure, although there was a subsequent disaster in December 1944 when lubrication was impeded by a blockage caused by cotton waste entering an oilway to the bearings.

The forward turbine proved to be far less troublesome and altogether more reliable than the reverse turbine, but its two failures were very costly and resulted in long stoppages of 64 and 147 weekdays in the shops. The first resulted in the coupled wheels becoming locked and was due to the movement of a stator diaphragm arising from temperature differentials between diaphragm plates. Subsequently there was an inwards movement of up to ⅛in, causing the diaphragm to come into contact with a row of turbine blades, stripping them off and damaging an adjacent row. In the repairs that followed the diaphragm was locked into its slot by using a keyed collar and the radial clearances of the moving blades were increased. The second failure took place at speed on an up journey from Liverpool when without any warning at all the screwed portion of the main turbine spindle under the thrust collar retaining nut fractured and allowed the turbine rotor to move laterally until the blades fouled. After this failure the turbine was returned to the makers for complete overhaul. No 6202 was in shops for 147 weekdays this time, and shortly after a return to traffic in August 1939, World War II broke out. This failure highlighted a major problem with any experimental and radically different locomotive when special components become defective – had there been a spare turbine a rapid change could have been effected and the stoppage kept to perhaps less than a month.

The failure of the slow-speed flexible drive occurred during a shed movement in 1943 when the coupled wheels locked. It originated in the flexible drive unit and was a consequence of normal wear in the driving pins and bushes connecting the gear wheel with the rotating link and driving axle, reducing clearances between the nuts securing the driving pins and the access holes in the gear centre disc so that they came into contact. The resultant knocking damaged the screw locking devices, nuts became loose, allowing slackness in the drive and transmission

of heavy shocks, particularly when changing direction. All of this led ultimately to the fracture of one of the pins and breakage of some high-speed pinion teeth. There was other damage to the flexible drive, including one of the axle driving arms. Twelve of the leaf springs in the left-hand side of the slow-speed gear wheel and three on the right had broken plates; out of 256 plates 68 were broken. After satisfactory repairs it was decided that this type of failure was best avoided by routine examination, a frequency of 10,000 miles being decided. No fewer than 378 weekdays elapsed before a return to traffic, but advantage of the stoppage was taken to give the locomotive a Heavy General Repair, including both turbines. Another failure caused a loss of 289 weekdays in 1946–7.

At times a severe loss of lubricating oil occurred, as much as 60 gallons in one instance, and sometimes small leakages persisted. Another source of trouble was aeration due to emulsification, because of the entry of condensed steam past labyrinth glands at the turbine bearings. The sump had no more than one minute's capacity when all three lubricating pumps were working, so there was no time in which oil settled and it therefore circulated in a more-or-less continuously frothy state in these conditions. In an attempt to overcome this the drain passages and oil return pipes were enlarged, drainage capacity was doubled and the exhaust steampipe from one of the steam pumps was clipped alongside the oil return pipe in order to reduce the viscosity. There was no improvement and the solution was to fit a larger reservoir which had internal baffles and a sloping bottom intended to separate the products of emulsification. The original tank was retained and fitted with a vent to assist de-aeration; existing oil drains and the high-pressure relief valve were connected into it. Tests found that the turbine gland ejectors did not create enough vacuum, so modified ejectors were obtained in order to reduce ingress of steam into the oil circuits. Oil loss and aeration was to remain the major source of uncertainty in the normal operation of the locomotive.

Other modifications related to the turbine drive included alterations to the control gear in 1937 and a new improved control box in 1939. At the 1937 overhaul ventilation louvres were fitted to the turbine casings.

Despite its radical transmission No 6202

conformed in many features to the rest of the class. Thus the frames from the intermediate coupled wheels to the rear of the locomotive were identical with those of the first two Pacifics and the front end was similar apart from the substitution of the turbine drive for cylinders. Unlike the rest of the class the brake pull rods were outside the frames. The boiler first fitted was similar to the rest of the 1935-built locomotives, having a larger superheater as described in Chapter 5, and when it was displaced by one with even more superheating in 1936 it was available for use with other members of the class. At times when No 6202 was out of service for prolonged periods the second boiler was also used on other 'Lizzies'. As both boilers were linked with the history of the rest of the class their history has been given in more detail in Chapter 5. Suffice it to add here that the second boiler, No 9236, which produced a superheat temperature of about 685°F, enabling a useful economy in coal and water consumption to arise, was slightly less efficient because of the higher smokebox temperatures; this in effect cancelled increased turbine efficiency derived from higher steam inlet temperatures. The balance was restored by fitting triple elements in place of the standard bifurcated type, although the steam temperature was not significantly more. The effect of this form of element was to increase resistance within the flue and therefore steam was able to absorb an adequate amount of heat from the gases. The point really proven was that to gain any advantage from a non-condensing turbine it was necessary to increase superheat, which even on No 6202 did not reach the maximum that could be attained on a conventional locomotive boiler without running into lubrication problems — if other events had not interfered would No 6202 have acquired a boiler similar to that planned for the two super Pacifics authorised for construction in 1940?

The smokebox was altered only to the extent that a double blastpipe and chimney were fitted, taking advantage of the reduced back-pressure arising from the turbine exhaust and to ensure adequate smokebox vacuum. Originally variable blastpipe caps were fitted, operated by a cam on the forward turbine steam valves control spindle, increasing or decreasing the area in relation to the number of valves open. This was done to meet the theoretical needs of the design but as so often happens right from the start it proved ineffective and an impediment to steaming. Therefore the caps were set in the minimum position, and steaming improved almost beyond recognition. At the earliest opportunity the apparatus was removed. The combined area of the two blastpipes was 31sq in and the smokebox vacuum was approximately 1in Hg for each steam valve open. The exhaust pressure varied from 1lb/sq in with two valves open to about 3lb/sq in with four valves open.

In turbine practice 'bleed' steam feed water heating is an established practice, so a feed water heater was provided situated transversely between the frames immediately behind the oil cooler, supplied with partially expanded steam from the forward turbine. It was in series with an exhaust steam injector which was located in the usual position below the footplate and could work with exhaust steam with a pressure as little as 1lb/sq in to deliver feed water at 190–200°F. The feed water heater increased the temperature to 275°F, resulting in a further economy of 3–4% in coal consumption.

Another difference, but not due to the turbine drive, was the use of Timken oil-lubricated roller-bearing axleboxes throughout the locomotive and tender. These proved to be extremely satisfactory, although they were an early application on Britain's railways. There were difficulties with local wear due to some of the outer races rotating within their housings; in the case of the bogie axleboxes steam was drawn into the bearings causing a slight pitting of the races and rollers, overcome by fitting an improved vent pipe. This particular trouble arose from the expansion and contraction of air within the boxes so that steam was drawn in and condensed on cooler areas.

In service the 'Turbomotive' gave a comfortable ride and the Motive Power Superintendent, Colonel H. Rudgard, stated that he found it so pronounced that it did not feel as if one were on a locomotive at all. It was generally found to have a dirtier than usual footplate on which to travel. There were complaints about signal sighting because of the lack of sufficient blast to clear the exhaust, so in July 1939 smoke deflectors were fitted. Another problem was caused by the continuous exhaust and absence of disturbing forces in the motion which made it difficult from the footplate to detect any slipping. To help drivers a speed indicator was fitted, driven from the left-hand trailing coupled wheel crankpin; when other locomotives on the LMS had their speed indicators removed during World War II the 'Turbomotive' alone retained its equipment.

Published weights varied and the three columns below show the anticipated weight when first planned, estimated weight given in the Press release in June 1935 and the final diagram which stated 'in working order':

Axle	Estimated tons	cwt	Press release tons	cwt	Final diagram tons	cwt
Bogie	19	3	19	4	21	6
Leading coupled	24	1	22	13	23	5
Intermediate coupled	24	4	24	0	22	8
Trailing coupled	24	3	24	0	23	6
Truck	19	17	19	3	20	6
TOTAL	111	8	109	0	110	11

The success of any experimental locomotive has to be judged by its availability for service and ability to do the job as well or preferably better than those it is intended to displace, for no experiment could be justified if the proponents did not have as a primary objective the introduction of their ideas in place of existing practices. It was seen that turbine propulsion offered something for main line express service where continuous steaming would ensure reasonable conditions for running a turbine, but it had to be accepted that for slow speed or local services a turbine drive had nothing to offer. Therefore experimental running could only be undertaken with 'top link' work and No 6202 must be judged on that basis. On pure mileage and availability statistics the locomotive must appear somewhat unsuccessful, with its low annual mileage and prolonged periods out of service. Thus up to 1945 the average annual figure was 28,500 (allowing for the time in store

from 1939 to 1941); the corresponding figure for the Princess Royal class was 53,000 miles, although they were capable of 80,000 in pre-war days. In fact in 1936–8 'Turbomotive' had averaged 54,205 miles per annum, reaching over 73,000 in 1936, a very satisfactory figure for an experimental machine and far in excess of any other unconventional locomotive tried in Britain. Even with a small fleet of turbine drive locomotives there would have been a supply of major spares so that defects could have been dealt with on a component change basis which would have drastically reduced the time in shops, and annual mileages would have been much closer to other locomotives.

The fact has to be faced that throughout the history of the steam locomotive in Britain any attempt to produce something radically different from the normal operating stock of a railway had no chance of success unless it did not make it so unusual and specialised that it could be accepted as an everyday tool for the job. No 6202 came nearer to success than any other because this fact was understood by its proponents who made it as near as possible compatible with existing locomotives.

Apart from the periods out of service due to major defects the 'Turbomotive' did not run from 21 September 1939 until 24 July 1941 because it was withdrawn from traffic due to its need for specialised individual attention, which was incompatible with dealing with our European enemies. For that period the locomotive was stored in the Paint Shop at Crewe Works, but the demand for large motive power was so great that a return to traffic to help with the war effort was necessary.

CHAPTER 5

THE PRINCESS ROYAL CLASS – MODIFICATIONS, AND THE 1935 BATCH

The first noticeable change to the class was the appearance of the second locomotive with a double blastpipe and chimney in October 1934 — no satisfactory reason has been established, but it could have been an attempt to improve steaming. The chimney itself was very plain as shown in the illustration and presumably no more than a temporary affair pending the outcome of the trials. What was curious in British practice was the separate discharge of the inside cylinders through the front blastpipe nozzle, with the outside cylinders discharging through the rear, a layout that was found to be disastrous. Five years later the Great Southern Railways of Ireland used the same arrangement on its new 800 Class 4–6–0 three-cylinder locomotives with complete success! This suggests that the fault was not in the separate exhausts, but in the tube arrangement itself. No 6201 was hastily altered to a single blastpipe and normal chimney. Efforts to improve the steaming of Nos 6200/1 initially centred round the type of element used rather than change the number of elements. The original elements were simply out and back loops in pairs (so giving 32 in 16 large tubes) and variations tried consisted of one having small tubes for the outward pass and a single large bore return, another with a lagged return tube and others of various diameters, most of which had 'downcomers' of much larger bore than the rest of the element. However it soon became evident that the solution was an altogether bigger

No 6201 *Princess Elizabeth* as fitted with an experimental double chimney in October 1934. It was soon removed. *LMS.*

superheater. The partially completed boiler intended for No 6202 was therefore fitted with a 32-element superheater, and it was installed on No 6200 in April 1935.

Early visual changes to Nos 6200/1 were the reduction in height of the vacuum pipe 'swan neck' on the front buffer beam and during 1935 the replacement of the original tenders by the more familiar pattern of the 4,000–gallon type (in May 1935 and March 1935 respectively). Two original features suppressed at an early date were the ashpan flushing equipment and the water de-sanding device which had proved unreliable and the latter very unpopular with the Signal Engineer. The next visual change was the appearance of a boiler with a dome which housed the regulator. No 6201 acquired the boiler which after removal from No 6200 had been modified with a 32-element superheater and dome in November 1935. The displaced boiler was then similarly modified and fitted to No. 6200 in June 1936. From then until 1952 these two locomotives used only these three boilers, two with a dome and one without, so that one or other ran at times domeless, the relevant dates being:

Until June 1936	Nos 6200 and 6201
June 1936 – May 1937	No 6200
September 1937 – February 1940	No 6201
April 1942 – November 1944	No 6200
November 1945 – July 1946	No 6201
September 1947 – July 1948	No 6200
November 1948 – February 1952	No 6201

The situation afterwards is described later.

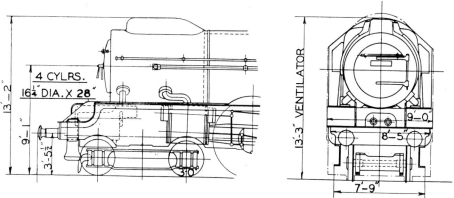

Fig 10 Streamlined cowl proposed for Princess Royal class chimney (1934). *British Rail.*

After work on the design changes to be applied to the ten locomotives built in 1935 had started, serious thought was given to streamlining and a 1:24 scale model was produced in March 1935 for wind tunnel tests. In appearance there was a strong resemblance to contemporary German practice, but the whole idea was dropped, no doubt because construction of the locomotives was well advanced, the first taking to the road only four months later. An early issue of the locomotive diagram showed a slight concession to streamling around the chimney by enclosing it in a form of cowl.

There were quite a number of changes in detail but visually, apart from the use of high-sided tenders, it was the boilers of Nos 6203–12 that showed most external change as the barrel was shortened and the firebox enlarged by its extension forward in the shape of a combustion chamber. This change is easily visible as the joint between the barrel and the firebox coincided with the trailing coupled wheels centre line rather than the trailing edge of those wheels. Structurally the boiler barrel was identical in the first and second rings, the third being shortened to match the longer firebox; consequently the tubes were 15in shorter, and this was a primary objective of the change. The fourth short parallel ring of the original boilers was not perpetuated, the barrel joining directly onto the firebox throatplate, a half-section of the ring being used to join the barrel and the upper part of the firebox shell. Frame plates were of different thicknesses, although the distance between them remained the same (including the rearward extension), the main frames being 1⅛in, the outer hind frame plates ⅞in and the inner 1in. To accommodate the altered throatplate the rear end of the frames had altered curvature on both the top and bottom edges, following different radii as shown in the drawing; it was also found necessary to slightly alter the hind frame plates to match. There were some small changes to the frames in addition to altered thickness; they were deeper by a ½in between the bogie wheels and a ¼in shallower between the bogie and leading coupled wheels. Another change was the use of hollow axles.

The lesson of superheater size had already been learned and it was intended that 24 elements would be used, but of the ten boilers ordered for these locomotives the first was diverted to the 'Turbomotive' and finished with 32 elements. The next four were finished with 24 elements and fitted to Nos 6203–6, but the last five had the enlarged superheater of the first of the batch. The four boilers with 24 elements were later modified to have 32 elements and details of tube

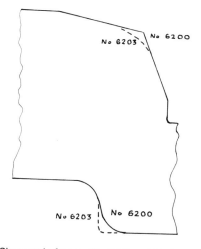

Fig 11 Changes in frames No 6200 and 6203.

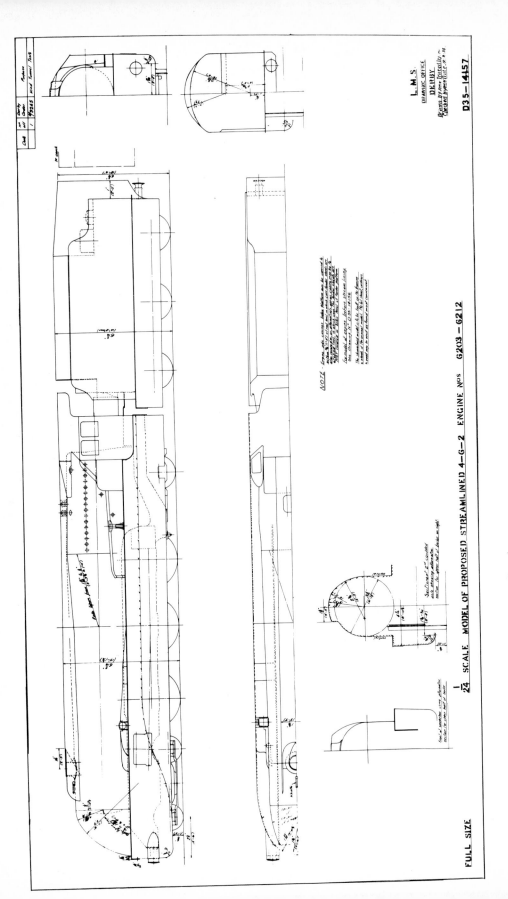

Fig 12 Streamlining proposals for the Princess Royal
class, 1935. *National Railway Museum.*

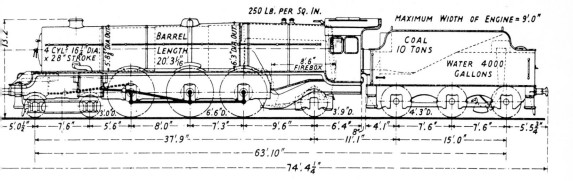

rrangements are given in Table 5. It seems that the 32 element boiler fitted to No 6202 was to have had 114 fire tubes instead of 112 as completed, and perhaps the 24 element boilers were to have had 143, being finished with 141. The suppression of two tubes occurred on many of the Stanier boiler types, extra washout plugs being inserted instead, an alteration to be found on several boiler types on many railways in Britain and Ireland after the first few had entered service. Two spare boilers were also built, both with all joints welded, unlike the rest which were conventionally rivetted. One was domeless like the rest and was fitted to No 6212 to compensate for the diversion of the first to No 6202, but the other was completed with an even larger superheater with 40 elements, and a dome housing the regulator and was used to displace the boiler fitted to No 6202, the latter then becoming a spare for Nos 6203–12. When the 'Turbomotive' was out of service for long periods its boiler was used on No 6210 from September 1943 to August 1944 and on No 6204 from August 1950 to April 1952 so for those spells both appeared as domed locomotives. With the enlarged superheaters a change was made to bifurcated elements in which the pipe down from the header was split into two, each of which then made one backward and one forward pass before combining again.

There were several other changes in detail on Nos 6203–12. Thus the arrangement of steampipes within the smokebox was altered at their joints with the inside cylinders in an attempt to ease the bends. When cylinder renewals for Nos 6200/1 were needed they also received this version. The 1935 locomotives had two 12-feed mechanical lubricators, one each side, supplying the cylinders and motion; later the first two locomotives were altered to suit when new cylinders were fitted. Another change was the

Fig 13 Princess Royal class Nos 6203 – 6212. *The Railway Gazette.*

provision of an eight-feed mechanical lubricator on the right-hand platform to supply the coupled axleboxes (two rams being spare). The GWR pattern 'rabbits ears' slidebars of Nos 6200/1 were not repeated, and Nos 6203–12 had standard LMS slidebars. The motion brackets were quite different, passing outside the slidebars on Nos 6203–12 instead of behind as on Nos 6200/1, but otherwise the motion was generally similar. An interesting innovation was the use of needle bearings in parts of the motion and ball bearings to the return cranks. However it was necessary to alter the reversing gear reach rods and the intermediate double-arm shaft had to be placed further forward, just ahead of the trailing coupled wheels splashers, instead of just to the rear, because of the extended firebox. The longer rod between the cab and the intermediate shaft had to be supported alongside the firebox by a bracket with a bearing surface on which it slid, the under-surface of the rod being shaped so that there was always contact as it moved.

An immediately noticeable change was the shape of the chimney, which had an almost continuous curve from the base to the lip with only a very short parallel section, unlike those on Nos 6200/1 which had a longer parallel section and sharper radii. Evidently someone at Derby was not convinced of the superiority of the chamfered mating faces of the smokebox door and the centre dart locking, as No 6212 appeared with a door which reverted to pre-Stanier practice with eleven locking lugs round its perimeter – later a standard door was fitted. Another visual change was the enclosure of the boiler feed pipes within the boiler clothing in their vertical section from below the platforms up to the top feed; on Nos 6200/1 they stood somewhat proud, being copied from Swindon practice.

The crosshead-driven vacuum pump was retained on Nos 6203–12 but standard LMS pattern driver's brake valves were used — both large and small ejectors were fitted. The brake valve handle movement was crosswise instead of to-and-fro as on Nos 6200/1 (and on No 6202 as built). Mechanical trickle sanding was retained, but without the water de-sanding device. The ashpan flushing arrangement tried on Nos 6200/1 was not repeated on the 1935 locomotives.

The early major modifications have been mentioned. The various tenders attached are described in Chapter 7, but it should be added here that No 6206 was modified with a steam feed to the tender so that the coal pusher fitted in its 1936 tender could be operated, being the only 'Lizzie' that could work such a device.

The four boilers built with 24-element superheaters were all converted to 32-element superheaters in 1943–51, individual *boiler* dates being given in Table 5. The locomotives which ran with the smaller superheaters were:-

No 6203 New – November 1936; November 1938 – October 1941; June 1944 – September 1947.
No 6204 New – January 1938.
No 6205 New – December 1940; October 1942 – December 1944.
No 6206 New – June 1937; July 1945 – August 1950.
No 6207 August 1937 – October 1943.
No 6208 April 1940 – August 1942; March 1948 – July 1950.
No 6209 February 1937 – September 1938; July 1941 – September 1943.
No 6211 February 1938 – October 1939; July 1942 – April 1944.

Eventually the major change to all locomotives of the Princess Royal Class was the alteration of all boilers so that the header regulator was replaced by one in a dome. At the same time a new style top-feed cover replaced the dome-shaped cover originally used. The new dome was placed on the third ring of the barrel. Boilers were in fact 'rebuilt' and not new, the relevant dates being given in Table 5. Nos 6200/1 were further modified so that they could take any of the fifteen boilers available, the change having been authorised as early as October 1941, but nothing was done until 1952. Compared to other Stanier

classes the changes to take the later pattern boiler were quite limited, affecting feedpipes and platforms and the cab front where the different widths of the fireboxes made small alteration necessary. A pocket had to be provided in the clothing of the later boilers to accommodate the reversing gear intermediate shaft on Nos 6200/, and the ashpan modified slightly because of the different shape of the hind extension frames. In fact once so altered neither No 6200 nor No 6201 ever had their original boilers again. Even fewer changes were needed when any of Nos 6203–1, ran with one of the original boilers; the first to have one was No 6208 in August 1950. With interchangeability established, locomotives ran with domeless boilers at the following dates:

No 6200 Until September 1956 ⎫ See *ante* for
No 6201 Until July 1954   ⎬ changes before 19
No 6203 Until September 1955 ⎭
No 6204 40-element boiler in August 195 (ex-No 6202) and always had domed boiler afterwards
No 6205 Until July 1952
No 6206 Until February 1955
No 6207 Until November 1955
No 6208 Acquired domed original type boile in August 1950 and always had domed boiler afterwards
No 6209 Until July 1956
No 6210 Until January 1953
No 6211 Until November 1952
No 6212 Until October 1952

After the loss of the rebuilt No 6202 in 1952 it boiler became available and was used on No 621 from January 1954 and then on No 6208 from January 1960, still having its larger 40-element superheater. Once interchangeable the three original boilers appeared on the following locomotives:

No 6204 May 1952 to withdrawal
No 6208 August 1950 to January 1957
No 6210 November 1955 to withdrawal
No 6211 July 1958 to withdrawal
No 6212 October 1952 to December 1953

A major change applied to only one of the class was the alteration of the valve gear and motion of No 6205 so that all four piston valves were driven by the two outside sets of motion; the motion brackets were very substantial, almost clumsy

This was an adaptation of Swindon practice with the major difference that it was the outside motion that drove the valves, whereas the GWR method was the reverse. No 6205 was altered in March 1938 and it was an expensive modification, costing £1,164. In May 1941 the Locomotive Committee minutes recorded that the change was satisfactory (although there were others who thought quite the opposite) but that it was not desirable in the conditions then prevailing to convert the remainder – perhaps a hidden way of saying that it was not really worthwhile!

What amounted to a rebuilding of some locomotives, but not regarded as such by British Railways, was the fitting of new front-end frames to Nos 6200/1/3/5–7/10/1 in 1952–4 at the dates shown in Table 1. No 6203 was so treated at Derby, the only time that an LMS Pacific was shopped there. Complete new sections were produced, incorporating cast-steel inside cylinders (having cast-iron liners) and when one of the class arrived in Crewe Works (or at Derby for No 6203) and found to be in need of such attention, the old section of the frames was cut off and the new immediately welded on. Even then there was still trouble with movement of outside cylinders and from 1953 'shear strips' were welded onto the frames, the cylinders having been removed, all the bolt holes on the cylinder and in the frame filled up, new bolt holes drilled and the strip annealed before its mating face was machined. On the cylinder the mating flange was also machined, and after the cylinder had been fitted a key of light interference fit was driven home and welded. Fracture of the weld indicated cylinder movement.

A multitude of other modifications were made over the years, some visible, others hidden. With hindsight the need or value of some was questionable and many really were only intended to benefit the workshops, having no value to the motive power department. Lesser changes made to boilers were the provision from 1936 of a continuous blowdown which discharged 1–1½ gallons of boiler water per minute so removing accumulated scum from the water surface. Originally the discharge passed into the tender but in 1951 a start was made on substituting a discharge pipe which fed into the ashpan. In an attempt to keep the boiler tubes cleaner and save time on shed it was decided in 1941 to insert a sand gun into the firebox backplate; fed by a hopper placed above it, a jet of sand controlled by a steam valve was blasted at the firebox tubeplate and into the tubes, being intended to dislodge clinker granules before they hardened and adhered to tube surfaces. Unfortunately one effect of this device, which was regarded as a diabolical contraption, was damage to the tubeplate and tube ends, so from 1952 the equipment was removed, having fallen out of use some time before. Changes affecting the boiler were modified feed trays which included a scoop arrangement, dating from 1941, and the removal of smokebox internal deflector plates (officially!) from 1942.

In 1936 all the locomotives had the mechanical trickle sanding replaced by steam sanding, Nos 6200/1 already having lost the de-sanding device. Brake equipment was hardly altered during the life of the class, but it was decided in 1938 to remove the crosshead-driven vacuum pumps as they were failing constantly and were expensive to maintain — in any case drivers usually kept the

No 46205 *Princess Victoria* with the modified valve gear fitted in 1938 (the separate inside valve gear was eliminated) *Real Photographs/Ian Allan.*

ejector open when running, so that the pump was doing nothing useful. Nos 6200/1 then acquired large ejectors as a consequence. It was not until 1945 that it was decided to eliminate the non-standard Gresham & Craven brake valves on Nos 6200/1 (and No 6202), but it was not until 1956 that all had been altered! Frames were modified slightly from 1939 to get increased side play in axleboxes and coupling rods for easier passage around six-chain curves in depots and sidings. Even as late as 1956 strengthened axlebox guides were found necessary, a change not completed until 1960. Bogies had to be altered by fitting different main springs (1948), stronger side control springs (1945), improved bottom frame bars (1948) and improved journal lubricating pads (1945). From 1944 improved pistons came into use — the fixing was altered to a screwed piston rod extension with right- and left-handed nuts with a locking plate between, and in consequence a new design of front cylinder cover had to be used. From 1954 steam-operated cylinders cocks replaced the original hand-operated type and their rodding. In order to detect overheating of inside big-ends a tell-tale device was introduced in 1950. Known to the staff as 'stink bombs' a capsule in the bearing disintegrated on excessive heating and emitted a strong garlic smell which could be sensed from the footplate, even at speed.

An early minor change decided upon in 1937 was to fit thicker glass (¼in) in cab windscreens. Cab wingplates were found to be weak and in 1939 it was decided to strengthen them. Blackout requirements of World War II made it necessary to fit screening to hide light emitted from the firehole and included plating over the fixed windows in the cabside. Another requirement of those dreadful days was the provision of containers for enginemen's respirators (gas masks) in accordance with Air Raid Precaution requirements.

Nowadays, some 50 years after the locomotives' introduction it is hard to believe that no form of speed indicator was fitted, nor anything resembling a form of warning system on the footplate. In daylight or darkness, in sunshine or storm, drivers relied solely on seeing for themselves oil-lit signals, some of which were far from ideally sited. It was not until April 1936 that it was decided to fit speed indicators and the Hasler pattern was chosen, driven off the left trailing crankpin. This equipment was apparently not too reliable, and in January 1938 BTH equipment was chosen as the standard to be fitted to nearly 1,000 LMS locomotives, the instruction to change to this type on the Pacifics being issued in July 1940. However it proved impossible to obtain them, let alone spares for those already fitted, and in June 1944 it was ordered that all fitted were to be removed. It was not until 1957 that British Railways resumed the fitting of speedometers, the type then chosen being a Smith's pattern with tacho-generator drive, again off the left trailing crankpin. The last change of any consequence was the fitting of the British Railways type Automatic Warning System (AWS) in 1957–8. Visible external fittings were the protection plate for the bogie-mounted receiver which prevented a swinging front coupling from damaging it, the vacuum reservoir on the right-hand side beside the trailing splasher, the timing reservoir on the left-hand side just in front of the cab and an equipment case just ahead of the cab on the right-hand platform, other fittings being inside the cab.

Once it had been ordered that the 'Turbomotive' was to be converted into a reciprocating locomotive design work was undertaken, and the outcome was a hybrid which had features of both the 'Lizzie' and 'Big Lizzie' classes — in effect a 6ft 6in version of the Coronation Class. The general details of the resulting locomotive were:

Main frames	– new, using a modified version of the Coronation type at the front end,
Inside cylinders	– cast-steel, Coronation type,
Outside cylinders	– cast-iron, Coronation type,
Motion	– new, Coronation type,
Coupled wheels	– originals, but machined and re-balanced,
Crank axle	– new,
Boiler	– existing Type 1 with sloping throatplate, modified with regulator in the dome,
Boiler mountings	– new superheater header and elements,
Smokebox and fittings	– new,
Cab	– original, modified to take reversing gear.

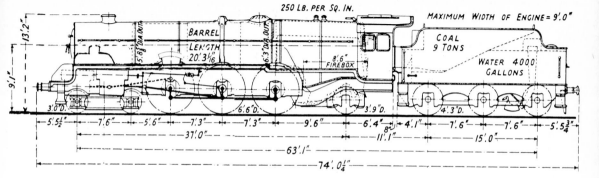

The boiler previously used by 'Turbomotive' was overhauled and fitted and by re-using many other compoments the finalised cost was kept down to £8,875 (by contrast, contemporary Britannia Class 7 Pacifics built for the London Midland Region cost £22,573).

At quite a late stage in the design a change was made that produced a noticeable difference – the open-ended platforms above the outside cylinders shown on the first issue of the locomotive diagram were altered so that the more traditional curved drop ends of the 'Lizzies' were used.

During 1952 permission was obtained to name the 'rebuilt' locomotive *Princess Anne*, after the Queen's daughter. Extremely unusual was the painting in the full green livery at the final stages of completion while still in the No 10 Erecting Shop at Crewe Works, but when all was ready No 46202 was hauled out just after noon on 13 August 1952. The original tender was ready, and coupled on later that day. Two days later No 46202 *Princess Anne* was sent out to Crewe North

Fig 14 The former turbine driven No 6202 as rebuilt with conventional drive in 1952 as No 46202 *Princess Anne*. This was the arrangement as carried out; original proposals envisaged first open end footplating between the two levels at the front end, and second the drop in the middle of the footplating between the leading and centre coupled axles. *Based on drawing in The Railway Gazette amended by the author.*

shed. Eight weeks to the day from leaving No 10 Shop No 46202 was totally wrecked in the dreadful collision at Harrow & Wealdstone on 8 October 1952. Covering only 11,443 miles there had been little chance to see how well this hybrid ran (although no adverse comment about its performance is on record) nor to judge whether or not it had any advantage over both LMS Pacific classes, thereby to justify the cost of its conversion.

No 46202 *Princess Anne* posed for the official photograph on completion of rebuilding in August 1952. *Crown copyright, courtesy National Railway Museum.*

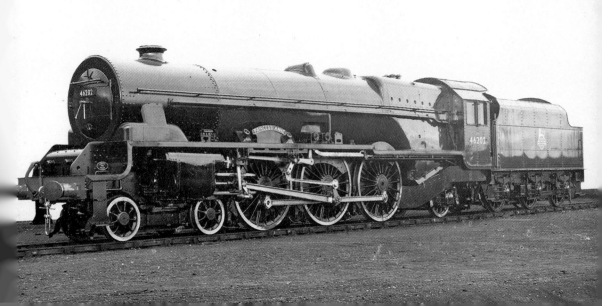

CHAPTER 6

THE CORONATION CLASS

Stanier's masterpiece, the streamlined Coronation Class, came about almost casually and certainly unexpectedly, for it was not until after the first batch had been ordered that a demand for a new high-speed luxury service between Euston and Glasgow made it necessary to design a new class suitable for the running performance planned. Thus in the summer of 1936 work went ahead preparing for the construction of more 'Lizzies'.

When production of the Pacifics authorised in July 1936 got under way no one expected that they would be other than five more of the Princess Royal Class — indeed, their numbers, 6213–7, were added to existing drawings and a start was made on the ordering of materials. These numbers were also quoted in the Locomotive Committee minutes, a rare distinction for locomotives on order. While awaiting authority for their construction Derby drawing office gave some thought to revised proportions for the Type 1 boiler and the following proposals were considered in April 1936:

Tubes			Type of element	Superheater			
No	dia in	Heating surface		No	dia in	SWG	Heating surface
116	2¾	2432sq ft	Bifurcated	32	1⅛	11	546sq ft
32	5¼		Triple	32	1	13	729sq ft
119	2⅝	2393sq ft	Bifurcated	32	1	11	546sq ft
32	5⅛		Triple	32	1⅛	13	729sq ft

Another form of elements, of 1⅛in outside diameter, called 'specials' (no other detail appears on record) was considered which in a 32-element superheater would give a heating surface of 510sq ft. The triple elements split the steam into three streams which each made backward and forward passes before re-combining, whereas the bifurcated elements split into two streams. The grate area and firebox heating surfaces were to remain the same as the 1935 boilers at 45sq ft and 217sq ft respectively.

It is quite clear from locomotive diagrams that were prepared that thought was given to varying the design of the 'Lizzies' and the major change was to shorten the coupled wheelbase to 14ft 3in equally divided, and reduce the total locomotive

and tender wheelbase from 63ft 10in to 62ft 10in, the 1ft 0in reduction consisting of 9in off the coupled wheelbase and 3in less between locomotive and tender. In appearance the locomotive would have seemed rather heavy at the front end as the boiler was unaltered and therefore the smokebox would have been closer to the front buffer beam. Locomotive projected weight in this form was 105 tons 16cwt. In fact sixteen years later No 46202 *Princess Anne* was virtually this proposal taking to the road! An alternative boiler with a firebox 6in shorter was also considered, perhaps to retain a front end which would have looked more like the existing Pacifics.

The success of the high-speed runs of a 'Lizzie' during 1936, spurred on by LNER performance on the East Coast route with Gresley A4 streamlined Pacifics, led to a re-think over the specification for the locomotives on order so that they could match the proposed train service requirements. Thus it was decided that the coupled wheel diameter was to be increased to 6ft 9in, no doubt influenced by the fact that the company already used that size for its Royal Scot, Patriot and Jubilee classes; it was close to the 6ft 8½in of the GWR Castle Class and the 6ft 8in of the Gresley Pacifics, it not then being accepted generally that the smaller diameter coupled wheels were just as suitable for the fastest trains. Robin Riddles is on record as having persuaded Stanier to make the change, an action he very much regretted later. The instruction given to the drawing office was to scheme out the biggest boiler possible and it was found that by taking a little off the top corners of the Belpaire firebox that the barrel could be enlarged to no less than 6ft 5½in and still fit within the loading gauge. Having accepted the shortened wheelbase proposal, it was retained in the new scheme and by revising the layout of the cylinders and motion it was seen that two sets of valve gear could operate the four piston valves. To overcome valve-setting problems arising from attaching the rocker arms at the outer ends of the piston valves it was decided that they should be attached between the value guides and the steamchest covers. This in turn made it necessary to place the outside cylinders further forward, which proved to be an advantage as the leading flange of the outside cylinders could overlap the rear flange of the inside cylinder casting so that the frames could be far more rigid at the point which was so often the weakest in three- or four-cylinder designs. When the time came for Stanier to decide on the layout of the new locomotives he was offered cylinder and valve gear schemes based on the existing Princess Royal Class and the new idea as well as the bigger boiler. He must have made his choice very quickly, selecting the scheme with the two sets of motion. He accepted the reversal of Swindon practice without apparently even requesting an alternative using inside motion, so far had he traversed the road away from Swindon without abandoning practices that were beneficial to the LMS. By this time streamlining was accepted as part of the design and Stanier then decided that the numbers should be 6220–4. The drawing office then had to cancel the material ordering sheets already in progress for Nos 6213–7 and start the process for the new class.

The stage was now set for an entirely new type of locomotive, streamlined to meet the dictates of prevailing fashions in travel, but time was short as less than one year remained in which to design,

construct and run-in before the new service was to start! Stanier became involved in the Pacific Locomotive Investigation Committee which had to seek the causes and recommend solutions to riding and derailment problems suffered by 4–6–2s running in India, which meant that he was away from England in the sub-continent when most of the design work was undertaken at Derby, but so well had he delegated that preparations proceeded smoothly and undisturbed. The final shape of the streamlining was determined after tests in the wind tunnel by the company's Research Department at Derby. In form the casing took a bulbous rather than the wedge-front shape adopted by the LNER for its streamlined locomotives.

In describing the construction details emphasis is placed on the differences between the two classes of LMS Pacifics. With the 'Big Lizzies' considerable effort was made to keep the weight of components down. After their introduction a very informative paper was published in *The Railway Gazette* during 1938 under the title 'The Metallurgy of a High Speed Locomotive', describing and comparing the results of using

No 6225 *Duchess of Gloucester* showing the recess for the drawhook and the steps on the front casing. Compared with the first batch, air vents have been incorporated in the casing just ahead of the inside cylinders. *LMS, R. T. Ellis collection.*

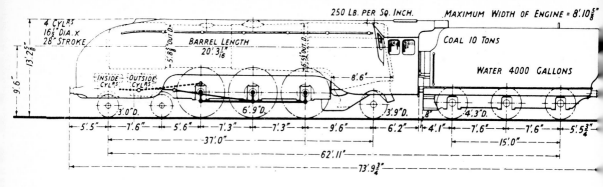

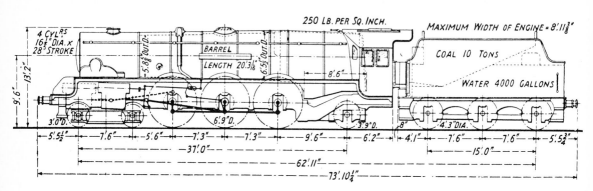

(*top*) Fig 15 Coronation streamlined 4–6–2. *The Railway Gazette.*
(*above*) Fig 16 Coronation non-streamlined 4–6–2. *The Railway Gazette.*

alternative metal alloys to the usual steels, etc.

The cylinders were of cast iron (a change being made to cast steel with cast-iron liners for renewals from 1952) and both inside and outside were inclined at 1 in 50. Having the same stroke as the 'Lizzies', the diameter was increased by ¼in to compensate for the larger coupled wheels. Exhaust passages in particular were designed to give the steam a free route, but not to enlarge the volume so much that they could act as receivers.

The exhaust from all four cylinders combined into a single blastpipe with a nozzle of 5¾in diameter, 3ft 0½in below the chimney throat which was 1ft 4½in diameter. Nos 6220–34 were so built, but after the trials with No 6234 in February 1939 (see Chapter 8) a double blastpipe with two 4⁷/₁₆in nozzles placed 1ft 3in below the boiler centre line was adopted. Nos 6235 onwards were built with that arrangement, the earlier locomotives being altered at the dates given in Table 2. No 6245 when new had a Kylchap exhaust experimentally fitted, which was soon replaced by the standard arrangement. The origins of this fitting are somewhat obscure, but it

is reputed to have been obtained from the LNER at Doncaster Works (having also been in the hands of the Southern Railway's Eastleigh Works)! Then someone asked why *City of London* made a very different noise to the rest of the class, and so the fitting was promptly removed.

Piston heads were of standard LMS pattern, but a larger diameter piston valve of 9in was used; the piston valve heads had reduced thickness webs which saved 96lb on all four.

The adoption of only two sets of motion has been mentioned, the motion particulars being given in Table 8. This contributed to weight reduction, but there was a bonus in that it largely eliminated attention to inside motion which would have been difficult because of the lack of light due to the streamlined casing. Had inside valve gear been fitted then it is possible that provision of electric lighting might have become a necessity.

A curious reversion to a practice already officially abandoned was the provision of Fowler-Anderson by-pass valves, which should never have been used – a Directors' minute of July 1934 ordered that they be discarded, for they were all too frequently the cause of total failure when the valve broke and allowed both ends of a piston to receive steam simultaneously! No doubt someone in the Derby drawing office was still fondly nursing feelings of pre-Stanier superiority of things Midland. Only Nos 6220–4 were built with them, No 6224 retaining them until condemned, although no doubt blanked-off.

Lubricating equipment was generally similar to the Princess Royal Class.

Although 2ft 0in longer than those of the 'Lizzies' the outside connecting rods were each 7lb lighter; including 47% of the weight of these rods, the weight of outside reciprocating parts to be balanced was 673lb per cylinder (676lb in the older class). The actual weight of the connecting rods were 366lb and 373lb for the two classes. For the inside motion, including 40% by weight of the inside connecting rods, the reciprocating weight per cylinder was 640lb compared with 715lb. The fluted section coupling rods were of the same grade steel and a saving of 412lb was achieved, the total weight of four rods being 908lb, but some of this reduction was obtained by shortening the coupled wheelbase. With a consequent reduction in weight of the revolving parts and of the actual balance weights themselves, there was a total saving of about 1,000lb in the valve gear and motion.

The first five locomotives were built with crosshead-driven vacuum pumps but in late 1938 it was ordered that they be removed.

The reversing gear was much simpler than on the 'Lizzies' and consisted of only the one weighbar shaft between the leading and intermediate coupled wheels, needing only the two arms for the outside valve rods. The reversing screw on the left-hand side of the footplate was connected directly to the weighbar shaft by a reach rod running just below the platform.

Crossheads, slidebars, motion brackets and other valve gear details were similar to Nos 6203–12.

Apart from their diameter, the coupled wheels were similar to those of the 'Lizzies' and all axles were bored out, the bogie axles having a 2in hole, the leading coupled and Bissell truck axles 3in and the intermediate and trailing coupled 4½in, saving in all 9cwt, the total weight of axles being 4¼tons. The coupled wheels were balanced to 50% of the reciprocating masses, equally divided between the coupled wheels; the whole of the revolving parts were balanced in each wheel.

Frame plates were 1⅛in thick, spaced 4ft 1½in apart and like the 'Lizzies' had the rear extension section with both inner and outer frames. The main frames were braced by the front buffer beam and dragbox, the inside cylinders, bogie bearer stretcher, smokebox saddle, a horizontal flanged tray adjacent to the saddle, a vertical stretcher between the leading and driving coupled wheels, another one between the rear pair of coupled wheels and a stretcher at the junction with the sliced frames, which also provided the pivot for the Bissell truck. Above the rear end of the front horizontal tray and rearmost vertical stretcher there were bearing surfaces for the boiler support saddles, which allowed for movement of the barrel. The extension frames overlapped the main frames on the inside, the outer plate extending as far as the horn guides of the trailing coupled wheels and terminating between the flange of the horn guide and frame plate, but the inner plate stopped at the horn guide. The extension was braced by a stretcher above the truck axle between the inner plates and between each pair of plates by another stretcher which included the trailing truck side bearers and the rear dragbox and buffer beam. In each vee of the extension plates there were further stretchers.

The choice of steel for the frame-plates was made after an investigation into the composition and quality of various special steels with particular reference to welding and oxy-acetylene or oxy-coal gas cutting. The grade chosen had 0·2% carbon, 0·85% manganese and 0·45% chromium, with other elements in minute quantities and was designed to avoid excessive local hardening when cut or welded. Even so, precautions had to be taken such as cutting at slower than normal speeds and re-tempering edges with a blowpipe and pre-heating areas to be welded where accessible, or welding at a slow speed. As plates ⅛in thinner were used there was a saving of 17cwt on a pair of frames compared with the older locomotives.

Springs were of standard LMS pattern silico-manganese laminated steel plates and they were attached to the axleboxes and carried on spring brackets as described beforehand.

Locomotive and tender were both steam braked, the former having a 10½in diameter cylinder carried on the frame stretcher between the rear pairs of coupled wheels. The brake blocks were applied to the front of each coupled wheel, having one block per hanger (some locomotives later had 'articulated' brake blocks

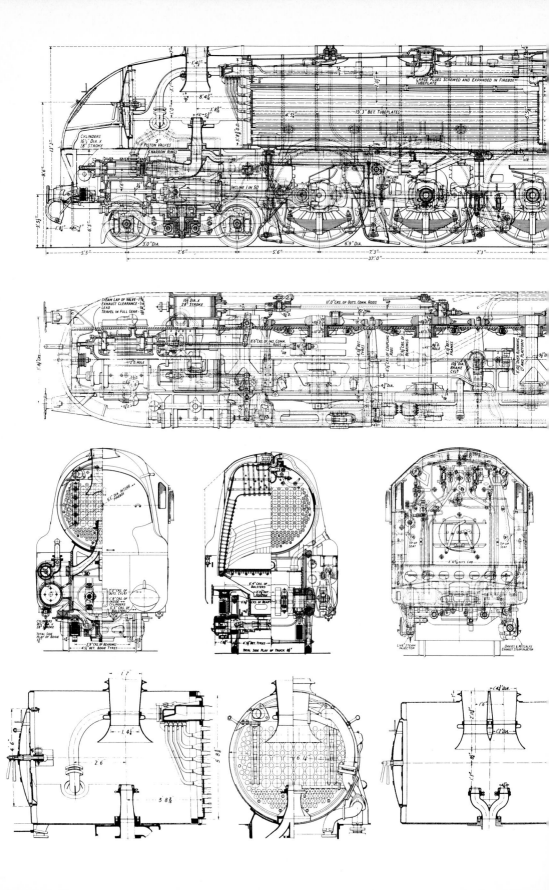

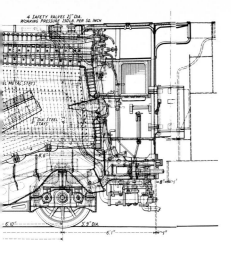

4 SAFETY VALVES 2½" DIA.
WORKING PRESSURE 250 LB. PER SQ. INCH

so that there were two blocks per hanger). The brakes were released by a pull-off spring, which unusually for LMS locomotives stood vertically, being anchored in the stretcher that carried the brake cylinder. The braking percentage for locomotive and tender was 51% for both streamlined and non-streamlined versions. Both the large and small ejectors were mounted alongside the smokebox and discharged through a waste pipe which entered the smokebox and turned up into the chimney petticoat.

Axleboxes were of the pattern imported by Stanier as described for the 'Lizzies' — they were lubricated in the same manner.

The leading bogie was identical with that used on the Princess Royal Class and the Bissel truck was also the same, being anchored 6ft 10in ahead of the axle centre line.

Locomotive hammer-blow, calculated at five revolutions per second, was:

Each pair of coupled wheels   1·31 tons,
Total for locomotive   0·24 tons.

Drawgear and buffers were standard LMS types, with the intermediate gear identical to that of the 'Lizzies'.

The boiler was rather bigger than that of the Princess Royal Class, being of the same diameter at the front, but 2½in greater in diameter at the throatplate, the firebox having a grate with 5sq ft more area and 13sq ft more heating surface. The boiler barrel and firebox wrapper plates were of 2% nickel-steel, allowing them to be thinner, the firebox being of the customary copper.

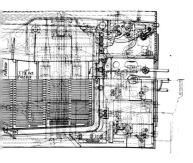

above and far left) Fig 17 Coronation class general arrangement drawing. *The Railway Gazette*.
left) Fig 18 Cab layout, Coronation class. *The Railway Gazette*.
below left) Fig 19 Single and double chimney layout. Coronation class. *The Railway Gazette*.

below) Bogie for No 6220 showing bar frames, plate equalisers and cup-shaped side bearers. *LMS, J. B. Radford collection*.

Compared with the normal grade of carbon steel there was a saving of 2 tons 3¼cwt by using nickel-steel, the empty boiler being 28tons 3½cwt. The comparison of plate sizes and weight saved were:-

	Thickness		Weight
	Nickel-steel	Carbon-steel	saved
First ring of barrel	5/8 in	13/16 in	12 cwt
Second ring of barrel	11/16 in	7/8 in	14 cwt
Throatplate	3/4 in	7/8 in	3 cwt
Firebox wrapper	1/2 in	5/8 in	9 cwt
Backplate	9/16 in	5/8 in	1¼ cwt

Unlike the Type 1 boiler on the Princess Royal Class the barrel on the 1X boiler was a frustrum of a cone (on the 'Lizzie' boiler the lower portion of the barrel was horizontal, although the upper portion tapered continously from smokebox to firebox; Type 2 and 2A boilers were similar but all the other Stanier taper boilers had a parallel front ring and tapered back ring). The front 9in, the section of the joint between the two rings (overlapping by 5¾in) and the final 1ft 4in at the throatplate end of the rear ring were parallel, to make assembly easier. The front tubeplate was recessed 7⅛in into the barrel and the throatplate consisted of a top and a bottom section; the top part joined the barrel to the firebox wrapper and formed the shoulders of the Belpaire firebox and the lower part formed part of the combustion chamber extension of the firebox, the joint between the throatplate and wrapper being at an approximate angle of 60°. The wrapper itself was a single plate and the firebox was of the maximum width possible, 7ft 9in at the throatplate, tapering to 6ft 11¹⁄₁₆in at the footplate end. The foundation ring gave a water space of 3¾in all the way round. The length of the firebox was 8ft 6in, the grate having a vertical drop of 1ft 4in, the level section at the backplate being 2ft 11⁹⁄₁₆in, the rest then sloping downwards to the throatplate where there was a final flat length of 5in. At this point the bottom of the foundation ring was 2ft 6¼in lower than the barrel at its joint with the throatplate. At the firehole the copper and steel backplates were flanged and rivetted together, being sloped forward, but above crown level the backplate was vertical. Slightly to the left of the vertical centre line there was an aperture for the sand gun which was fitted from new. Both the firebox crown and roof were sloped from the throatplate at 1 in 21·841 to the backplate, the maximum height of the boiler being 3ft 4in above the centre line, the back corners being 2ft 10in above the centre line. The staying of the firebox crown and water spaces comprised ½in steel stays, except in the areas of greatest expansion where ⅝in Monel metal stays were used, and rivetted except in the fire area where they were nutted inside the firebox.

To give the boiler longitudinal strength there were end-to-end stays from tubeplate to backplate, a distance internally of 30ft 5⁵⁄₁₆in, with shorter stays at each end to connect the tubeplate with the first ring and the backplate to the second ring. There were also cross stays above the firebox crown. The water space increased from 3¾in at the foundation ring to 5in at the backplate end of the firebox crown and 5⁵⁄₁₆in below the combustion chamber. For inspection and cleaning purposes there were LMS standard mud-doors at each corner of the firebox and above crown level, with additional washout plugs. The smokebox was joined to the barrel by an external steel ring 2⁵⁄₁₆in deep rivetted to the parallel section of the barrel just ahead of the recessed tubeplate. Stiffening plates were fitted to each ring of the barrel, where the frames were fitted with supporting stays. A steadying bracket held the boiler at the throatplate, while it was restrained at the back end by a diaphragm plate.

The tube arrangement was 129 firetubes of 2⅜in outside diameter and 11 swg and 40 flue tubes of 5⅛in outside diameter and 7 swg, all 19ft 3in between tubeplates. Unlike the Princess Royal Class it was never necessary to have any other number of tubes.

The grate was built up in three sections, the rear being level, the rest sloping as earlier described. From No 6229 the front section consisted of two cast-iron frames which held cast-iron door portions, operated simultaneously from the footplate, their purpose being to assist fire-dropping as they were not really drop-grates in the usual sense. A full drop-grate was introduced after World War II and Nos 6253–7 had boilers built with them, other boilers being modified later. In contrast to the standard LMS cast-iron firebars, some boilers were fitted with Hulson pattern firebars which had a much smaller space betwen them. The firedoors were standard with the 'Lizzies'.

The cast-iron superheater header in the smokebox fed 40 triple elements of 1in outside diameter and 11 swg, providing 120 paths for the steam. Subsequently the thickness of the element walls was altered and the differing heating surfaces are listed in the tables of dimensions.

The regulator was a standard LMS grid type with pilot and main valves, opened and closed by a rod fitted internally which passed through a stuffing box on the backplate. There were baffle plates below the dome to prevent water from lifting and passing into the main steampipe which was 7in internal diameter. The centre line of the dome was 12ft 4³⁄₁₆in from the extreme front of the barrel and the top feed was 6ft 5³⁄₄in nearer the front.

The ashpan was virtually in two sections, being divided to clear the trailing truck axle, and therefore very shallow at that point. There was a damper door at each end, separately worked from the footplate by links as described in Chapter 3. Later some boilers acquired a more positive screw and links to operate damper doors. From No 6225 ashpans were fitted with hopper doors in the two portions of the ashpan. Unlike the 'Lizzies', ashpans did not have side doors until the last pair was built in 1947-8 — there was no point as they were inaccessible under the streamline casing.

In the smokebox the steampipes were positioned well to the sides, making the bottom as clear as possible to facilitate the removal of ash. The junction for the inside and outside cylinders was outside the smokebox and on the non-streamlined version was covered in a distinctive bulbous casing. With the streamline casing the upper part of the smokebox was sloped to correspond, but on non-streamlined locomotives the smokebox had a fully circular shape. As with the Princess Royal Class the smokebox plates were a copper-bearing steel.

An exhaust steam injector was placed below the right-hand side of the footplate and a live steam on the left, both delivering directly to the top-feed clacks which discharged onto trays within the steam space so that any air in the feed separated. The feed then passed through a further pair of pipes which discharged below water level.

The four 2½in pop safety-valves, set at 250lb/sq in were mounted on top of the Belpaire firebox close to the backplate; they could not have been any further forward due to the loading gauge. The whistle lay horizontally just ahead of the safety-valves.

The footplate layout was generally very similar to that of the 'Lizzies' but the front of the cab was angled whether the locomotive were streamlined or not. On the streamliners the front lookouts

Head-on view of No 6234 *Duchess of Abercorn* showing the bulbous casing around the external steam pipes, hidden beneath the streamlining of the streamlined locomotives, or later obscured by smoke deflectors. *Real Photographs/Ian Allan.*

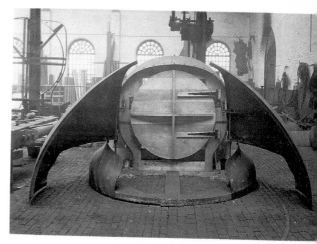

Former for the assembly of the streamlined nose prior to fitting on a locomotive. *LMS.*

No 6220 under construction, showing attachment of the streamlined casing. Note the hollow axle centres. *LMS, J. B. Radford collection.*

(which were not hinged) were rather on the small side, but otherwise the cab was no different.

Underneath the streamline casing the boiler was fully clothed in the way described for the 'Lizzies'. Those built without streamlining were likewise covered and in their case finished in the appropriate livery. The streamline casing was formed carefully on wooden jigs and then fitted on a light framework. At the front end the framework was rather stronger with a horizontal extension of the platforms as far as the rounded nose end. Below this extension the casing covered the cylinders and was shaped round the buffer shanks, having a plain opening for the front drawhook. There was a pronounced widening at the outside cylinders, and from No 6225 onwards ventilation louvres were added at this point. At the same time a small step below the front drawhook was added. The upper part of the nose opened-up to give access to the smokebox and inside valves; the shape of the doors can be seen in the illustration. The lower panels along the side of the locomotive had opening portions to give access to the mechanical lubricators, but the sandboxes had extension pipes with caps which were flush with the casing.

Speedometers were fitted to Nos 6220–4, having equipment supplied by Stones-Dueta, but afterwards BTH equipment was preferred and most built up to 1944 had those fitted. The first five soon had the BTH type fitted as replacements; the 1944 instruction to remove all speedometers has been mentioned in Chapter 5.

By the time that the 'Big Lizzies' were designed trickle sanding had been abandoned and steam sanding was fitted, applied to the front of the leading and intermediate coupled wheels and the rear of the latter. There were separate sandboxes for each position, fitted within the frames, having long filler pipes.

The details of dimensions given in Table show that less than three tons was added to the weight of the locomotive when streamlined.

The final version of the LMS Pacifics was designed to obtain comparative data on the latest developments in steam motive power, applying

The very last Stanier Pacific to be completed just missed being an LMS locomotive, being finished in the second month of Nationalisation as No M6257 *City Salford, J. B. Radford collection.*

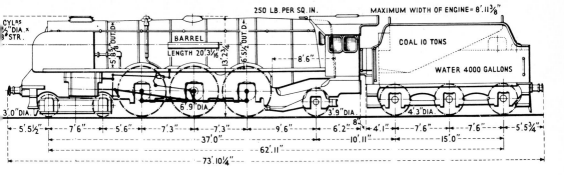

250 LB. PER SQ. IN.   MAXIMUM WIDTH OF ENGINE= 8'.11⅜"

CYLRS ¾"DIA. x ¾"STR.

BARREL LENGTH 20'.3¹⁶₁⁶

COAL 10 TONS

WATER 4000 GALLONS

8'.6"

5'.8⅜"OUT D.

13'.2¾"

6'.5½"OUT D.

3'.0"DIA.

6'.9"DIA.

3'.9"DIA.

4'.3"DIA.

5'.5½" — 7'.6" — 5'.6" — 7'.3" — 7'.3" — 9'.6" — 6'.2" — 4'.1" — 7'.6" — 7'.6" — 5'.5¾"

37'.0"

8'.

10'.11"

15'.0"

62'.11"

73'.10¼"

Fig 20 No 6256 with modified trailing end. *The Railway Gazette.*

lessons learned during World War II to aid servicing, and to add various design refinements in an effort to increase annual and shopping mileages. At the same time as the last two, Nos 6256 and 6257 were built, the company constructed the first two diesel-electric locomotives to work in main line service in the United Kingdom, Nos 10000 and 10001, and it was the intention to compare their performance with the two Pacifics on workings between Euston and Glasgow.

The design of these two Pacifics was generally similar to the earlier non-streamlined type and the innovations were the responsibility of Mr H. G. Ivatt, the last Chief Mechanical Engineer of the LMS. The aim was the 100,000 miles per annum locomotive (see Chapter 10) and externally there seemed to be relatively little change in appearance until looking closely at the trailing end where the extension frames and the truck were of new designs.

Perhaps the most important change was the use of grease-lubricated roller-bearing axleboxes on both the locomotive and tender. The crank axle of the leading coupled wheels had Skefco self-aligning boxes to accommodate the 'breathing' of the cranks. All the other boxes were Timken tapered roller bearings, those on the bogie, intermediate and trailing coupled axles being split-cannon type, the remaining axles having individual boxes. Associated with the roller-bearing axleboxes was the use of manganese-steel

liners on the axlebox and hornguide faces, a feature that already proved its value in raising the mileage between shops on other LMS types. It had reversed the situation whereby locomotives were shopped due to the condition of axleboxes and tyres — the life of other components consequently had to be improved to match. This feature was a direct import from America, the Timken company drawing Derby's attention to the practice. A further change was the use of frame clips ('Horwich' clips in the shops) across the horn gaps, which were light bars and very much easier to handle and fit than the previously standard 'keeps' which were extremely heavy to handle and fit.

The main frames terminated behind the trailing coupled axleboxes as on the original design, but instead of the spliced extension a 2in thick semi-bar frame was rivetted on, supporting the rear buffer beam. A pair of support brackets transferred the weight to a new design of trailing truck which comprised a one-piece cast-steel frame, known as a 'Delta' truck. Side control was by means of helical springs. One reason for the change was the need to make room for the redesigned ashpan. This ashpan was fitted with the arrangement of rocking grate adopted by the LMS and copied almost entirely from the gear fitted to the United States Army Transportation Corps 2–8–0 classes which ran in Britain in 1942–4. The grate consisted of two main sections side-by-side, divided into the front, middle and back parts; each section could be rocked during running by a short to-and-fro movement of the control gear on the footplate. By lifting a restricting bracket, the grate could be rotated by 90 degrees to dump the fire into the ashpan. The ashpan had hopper doors to discharge the fire. It also had the normal damper doors, but at last the means of control was improved, having a positive handwheel and screw instead of the notched levers.

An innovation was a new design of reversing screw and cut-off indicator. The screw itself was moved from the traditional position in front of the driver to a new location inside the frames adjacent to the weighbar shaft. It was coupled by a tube and universal joints to the handwheel in the cab, placed sideways instead of directly facing the driver so that it was easier to turn. The position of the gear was indicated on a drum attached to the handwheel and later the arrangement was adopted for British Railways standard designs.

The smokebox was fitted with wire mesh grids, easily removable for tube cleaning, which created a self-cleaning action. The boiler top-feed was of a new design, dispensing with the trays and relying on deflector plates in the form of a saddle over the tubes, intended to deposit sludge well clear of the tubes on the bottom of the barrel. However there was still a feed water de-aerating action.

Trailing end of the final pair, showing the Delta truck. Compared with the view when new the truck has been modified so that it appears as a made up structure rather than a single casting. The joints can be seen and compare the lightening holes in the truck frames. *J. B. Radford collection.*

The number of superheater elements was increased but the heating surface was enlarged the use of '5P4' elements which boosted heating surface to no less than 979sq ft. This for of element comprised a single 'outward' tu which split into four inside the flue tube and th returned as a single larger diameter central tu to the header. The four tubes were 1in diame and had external fins; the return tube was 1½ This form of element did not last long and v replaced by the standard 1in triple elements. new feature of the boiler was the use of a blow-cock on the throatplate, operated by a lever wit handle on each side of the locomotive. It was us on shed and kept open for one minute, purpose being to discharge some of the slud and scale from around the firebox.

Due to the redesigned trailing truck a frames the cab side sheets were reduced in dep lacking the curved front corners at the botto the similarities to the Ministry of Supply 2–8 locomotives soon earned the two Pacifics name of 'Austerity 4–6–2', virtually unknown the railway. The smoke deflectors and platfor at the front end were identical with those of t de-streamlined locomotives. Initially Nos 462 and 46257 were fitted with electric headligh with white markers for daytime use, but t equipment suffered a number of defects and w fairly quickly removed.

From Table 2 it will be seen that while the first of the pair is dated December 1947 the second did not appear until May 1948, although in fact it was ready in the February and was photographed officially as M6257. The delay arose from the performance of the trailing truck and a study of the two illustrations reveals quite substantial changes in construction. The initial form which looks quite tidy in the illustration was replaced by an almost makeshift looking frame with circular instead of triangular lightening holes. The axleboxes and the frame immediately around them were not altered. Nothing was ever admitted by officialdom to explain the need for the modification. Rectification and modification took up a considerable time in 1948, No 6256 being in Crewe Works for non classified repairs for the following dates:

16 February 1948 –13 May 1948
75 weekdays
8 June 1948 – 3 July 1948
23 weekdays
6 September 1948–25 September 1948
18 weekdays
9 October 1948 –16 October 1948
7 weekdays.

Despite this the mileages for 1947 and 1948 were 563 and 48,686, followed by 88,219 in 1949 which was the highest annual figure attained by this locomotive.

For the 'Lizzies' details of boilers were given in Table 5; the corresponding boiler orders and numbers for the 'Big Lizzies' were:

Order No	Boiler Nos	Allotted locomotives
B402	9937–41	6220–4
B414	10287–96	6235–44
B408	10297–10306	6225–34
B415	10637–46	6245–54
BS1/39	10693/4	Spares
B464	12470–4	6253–7
BS1/78	13043/4	Spares

When locomotive No 6229 was being prepared for the American Tour during construction a boiler was taken out of sequence, No 10306 being

No 6235 *City of Birmingham*, the first to have its streamlined casing removed. At first the original chimney was retained but it was replaced by a lipped casting before the locomotive went back into service. At this stage the smoke-deflectors were without toe-holes or hand grips, both added before re-entry to traffic. *LMS, J. B. Radford collection.*

fitted instead of No 10301, the latter and the next four being used on locomotives Nos 6230–4; otherwise locomotives Nos 6220–44 received boilers in sequence. On the outbreak of World War II locomotives Nos 6240–4 were well advanced and already fitted with their allotted boilers. The other ten boilers were in hand and two (Nos 10637/8) were used as replacements on locomotives Nos 6220/2 in December 1939. The next five boilers (Nos 10639–43) were later completed and used in 1941–3 on Nos 6231/32/38/23/36. When construction of the locomotives resumed Nos 6245/7/8 were fitted with second-hand boilers, Nos. 6246/9/50 got new boilers 10645/44/46 respectively and Nos 6251/2 received two ordered as spares (Nos 10693/4). The final batch of five received their boilers in order.

As with the Princess Royal Class several modifications were made to the Coronation Class; those which were applied as construction proceeded have been mentioned. The most important and obvious change was the removal of the streamlined casing and the fitting of smoke deflectors. Both changes were decided in December 1945, the first being to fit the deflectors to Nos 6230–4/49–52, although two, Nos 6232/52, had been fitted experimentally in February and March 1945 respectively in accordance with instructions issued in July 1944. The dates of fitting are given in Table 2. The removal of the streamlined casing started with the alteration of No 6235 in April 1946. Only No 6243 was not dealt with by Nationalisation, having to wait until May 1949. At the same time smoke deflectors were fitted and when the first was altered these did not have footholds or handholds, being quite plain, but holds were provided immediately as the shape of the platforms at the front end made their introduction urgent. When altered the platforms were not continuous at the front, lacking the traditional curved portion in front of the cylinders; the open gap was a concession to maintenance so that no time was consumed in having to remove the curved portion when attending to the valves. When Nos 6230–4/49–52 were fitted with smoke deflectors they soon acquired the handholds, but it was not until May 1955 that an order was issued to provide the footholds as they had the curved section of platform which included a footstep. When the first locomotive had its streamlining removed it was left with the plain chimney casing that had been used before, having no lip, but before entering service a new chimney with a lip was fitted. The sloping top to the smokebox remained unchanged until in 1952 a start was made on the substitution of a fully circular front when renewals were necessary. The dates of these changes are given in Table 2. After locomotives had been running de-streamlined for some years complaints were made about the smaller forward lookouts and eventually standard size front windows were fitted. Another change associated with the removal of the streamlining was the addition of the bulbous casing over the steampipes outside the smokebox – like 6230–4 – mostly obscured by the smoke deflectors.

Many of the lesser changes applicable to the 'Lizzies' were made to the 'Big Lizzies', such as alterations of the continuous blowdown, sand gun removal, frames and bogies, improved

No 46245 *City of London* at Old Oak Common shed o September 1964 on the occasion of the last working Stanier Pacific into London under British Railw ownership. The AWS receiver is protected fr damage by the screw coupling by the plate affixe the buffer beam. *Alec Swain.*

pistons, 'stink bombs', ARP requirements AWS. After the removal of speedometers in 1 thought was again given to fitting some with equipment in 1947, Nos 6256/7 being built v those fittings; a modified driving gear mounting were intended, but nothing was d until 1957–8 when Smith–Stone units w installed.

Following its extensive damage in Octo 1952 at Harrow & Wealdstone No 6242 retur to service with traditional shape platforms at front end, a feature which made it unique am the former streamlined locomotives.

A major alteration that was considered in de but never applied was a mechanical stoker; many locomotives were to be fitted was decided before all work on the project abandoned about 1952. Two American devi were given consideration, the Standard and Berkeley, but neither offered any econo advantage over conventional hand firing.

The last to remain streamlined, No 46243 *City of Lancaster*, stands in the works yard at Crewe on 7 May 1949. *A. G. Ellis.*

CHAPTER 7

TENDERS

oon after Stanier took office on the LMS the ubject of water capacities of tenders was liscussed by the Mechanical and Electrical Engineering Committee. It recorded at the meeting of 27 April 1932 that the best capacity for LMS routes was 3,500 gallons for general purposes, but if longer non-stop running or heavy haulage were involved larger tenders might be necessary. The Committee added that if more han 4,000 gallons were needed it would probably be cheaper to lay down extra water troughs. The West Coast route of the LMS was in fact well provided with water troughs, their distances rom Euston (in miles) being: Bushey 15½, Castlethorpe 54, Brinklow 84, Hademore 114, Whitmore 148, Moore 179, Brock 217, Hest Bank 233½, Dillicar 261, Floriston 306 and Strawfrank 371½.

The great majority of Stanier's tender engines were provided with 4,000-gallon tenders. One class, the Class 5P4F 2–6–0 of 1933–4 had the 'Old Standard' tender of 3,500 gallons (the type used by Derby under the Fowler regime) built for them and always used that type. Several of the Class 5XP 4–6–0 passenger engines ran, some from new, others later, with displaced 'Old Standard' tenders, or in the case of ten of them a straight-sided version (locomotives Nos. 5607–16 when new). There was a Stanier 3,500-gallon tender which had a slightly smaller version of the body used for the 4,000-gallon type. Allotted initially to Class 5XP 4–6–0s Nos 5617–66 they represented a short-lived adherence to the 1932 minute! It must have become apparent very soon that there was no point in the difference of 500 gallons nor in the effort needed to monitor the classes to which they were attached when tenders were exchanged.

The story of the tenders attached to the Princess Royal class locomotives is involved, three versions being used, but in the case of the 'Turbomotive' and the 'Big Lizzies' no changes took place after entering service. All the variations occurred in the tender body, the frames being standard throughout. In summary the body variations were:

(i) Original straight high-sided,
(ii) Standard version with curved coping,
(iii) Enlarged capacity of 10 tons of coal, which appeared in two shapes, the second being used with streamlined locomotives, and with or without a coal pusher.

Nos 6200/1 started life with version (i), then all of Nos 6200-12 had version (ii), followed by Nos 6200/1/3–12 acquiring non-streamlined version (iii). The Coronations always had version (iii), all with coal pushers; those that had streamline fairing lost it when the locomotives were de-streamlined. No 6206 of the 'Lizzies' also had a coal pusher tender. Details of dates of change of type are given in Table 9.

TABLE 9
TENDER DIMENSIONS AND NUMBERS

Mark	I	II	III	IV	V
Wheel diameter	4ft 3in	4ft 3in	4ft 3in	4ft 3in	4ft 3in
Coal	9 tons	10 tons	10 tons	10 tons	10 tons
Water	4,000 gal	4,000 gal	4,000 gal	4,000 gal	4,000 gal
Weight (empty)	27t 16c≠	27t 16c*	26t 16c	28t 10c	28t 10c
(laden)	54t 13c≠	54t 13c*	54t 13c	56t 7c	56t 7c

≠ Tenders Nos 9000/1 as built 11 cwt lighter.
* Tenders Nos 10623/4 17 cwt heavier.
The different tenders were:

Order No	Mark	Tender Nos	First locomotives	Remarks
T371	I	9000/1	6200/1	Replaced by Mark 1 Nos 9065/6
T378	I	9002	-	Initially intended for No 6202, but used for 1933 American Tour of No 6100 Royal Scot.
T371	I	9003	6202	
T390	I	9065/6	6200/1	Replaced by Mark III.
T395	I	9124-33	6203-12	Replaced by Mark III.
T398	III	9344/5/53/4	6200/1/3-12	10-tons replacements (not attached in numerical order).
T399	III	9359-61/72-6		
T402	IV	9703-7	6220-4	
T408	IV	9743-7	6225-9	
T408	V	9748-52	6230-4	
T414	IV	9798-9807	6235-44	
T415	IV	9808-11	6245-8	
T415	IV	9812-5	6249-52	Later listed as Mark II
T464	II	9816/7	6253/4	
T464	II	10622-4	6255-7	

At the time of condemnation No 6206 had tender No 9816 attached and No 6221 was shown with Mark I 9-ton tender No 9459; the latter was attached solely as a replacement so that a better tender was not scrapped with the locomotive.

Tenders Nos 9000/1 were replaced by Nos 9065/6 in May and March 1935 respectively and 10-ton tenders were attached to Nos 6200/1/3-12 in 11/36, 11/36, 1/37, 12/36, 5/36, 10/36, 12/36, 7/36, 10/36, 9/36, 6/36 and 7/36 respectively.

The tender frames had an equally divided wheelbase of 15ft 0in, the six wheels being 4ft 3in diameter when new. There was a single steam brake cylinder, which through the rigging applied the blocks to the rear of each wheel simultaneously with the steam brake on the locomotive. The original tenders (version (i)) had a braking percentage, based on two-thirds

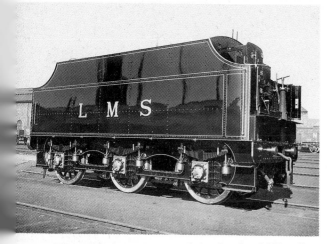

The original appearance of the Stanier 4,000-gallon tender, No 9000 of 1933, as new with roller-bearing axleboxes. *LMS, R. T. Ellis collection.*

quantities of coal and water, of 60 percent. The first of these two tenders was fitted with roller-bearing axleboxes, but it was not until the last two Pacifics were built in 1947–8 that such boxes were used again. The plain bearing journals were 7½in diameter and 10⅝in long. Main frames were 1in plates outside the wheels, extra strength being provided by a pair of ⅝in plates between wheels which acted as stays between the front and rear dragboxes; these plates were not quite as deep as the rear buffer beam. The main frame plates had lightening holes between the axles and were braced across the bottom by two horizontal stays, at each end by the dragboxes and at the top by two more horizontal stays and light vertical plates. The drawgear between locomotive and tender comprised a main drawbar on the centre line and a pair of secondary drawbars, one to each side. The intermediate buffers were 3ft 8in apart, having coil springs at the rear of the dragbox. At the trailing end of the tender standard buffers and drawgear were fitted. The water scoop was of the standard LMS type, hinged and held clear of the track except when lowered to pick up water; it also had a pair of deflector plates in front to channel water into the scoop. Water passed up a cast-iron trunk into the tank. The water scoop and the tender handbrake were operated by handles mounted on the vertical faceplate of the tender body, connected through bevel gearing. This layout was new to the LMS but was used on all Stanier tenders. It originated from the greater throw-over caused by the longer trailing length of

a Pacific design which made use of the vert pillars of the 'Old Standard' design undesirab

The design of the tender originally fitted to first two Pacifics (version (i)) was not actually r when it was decided that 4,000 gallons capac was needed. In outline, if not in more detail, tender design already existed but none had b built. As mentioned in Chapter 1 a tender of t capacity was shown on the weight diagr prepared for the proposed Hughes' version of heavy freight 2–8–2 in 1924. For the Pacifics major change was to increase the coal capacity nine tons instead of eight. So often in the past t type of tender has been described as a modif version of those used with Derby's pre-Stan classes, but it was wider and longer, being the t width of the locomotive cab. It was quickly fou that the bunker did not have acceptable se trimming qualities and the body design v modified to achieve this, the shape be considerably improved in appearance increasing the height of the sides and giving th an inward curve, so forming the well kno Stanier tender (version (ii). Three version tenders were built, the third ordered as that the third locomotive but attached instead to Cl 6P 4–6–0 No 6100 *Royal Scot* when it toured t United States of America in 1933. Afterwar that tender was modified to version (ii), as we the other two, and all three attached to new Cla 5P5F 4–6–0s in 1935. Access to the coal space w through a folding door in the faceplate, norma kept closed, coal being removed through the g between the lower edge of these doors and t bunker floor, which was extended slightly at t doorway to form a shovelling plate. A long tun was provided on the fireman's side of the body house fire irons. On the other side of the facepl a wooden lined compartment was provided f the enginemen to put away jackets and fo boxes.

To get a coal capacity of 10 tons the body w extended upwards to the maximum heig possible, but otherwise details were no differe from the 9-ton type, except when completed streamline form. As version (iii) a dozen of the tenders were built in 1936. No 9359, attached locomotive No 6206 was provided with a co pusher, possibly as a trial of the device before commitment to its use on the streamlin locomotives. Therefore no other Princess Roy could use this tender and operate the coal push as it required a steam supply to work it. Th

pusher consisted of a 10½in diameter piston in a cylinder mounted on the sloping floor of the bunker and it pushed two wedge-shaped rams down the slope. Steam for it was taken from the manifold on the firebox and fed through a flexible connection to an operating valve mounted on the tender faceplate, its operating lever being placed just inside the fire-iron tunnel. The pusher exhaust escaped at the top of a protective cover plate at the rear of the cylinder on the outside of the bunker backplate, although originally the exhaust was directed into the water tank.

For the streamlined 'Big Lizzies' the tender body side sheets were extended to the rear and

No 46201 *Princess Elizabeth* in British Railways lined black. This view illustrates features of the rear of the 10-ton tender. *BR.*

(*left*) Front end of tender No 9703 showing the coal pusher and its two rams at the back of the bunker. At the mouth of the left-hand tunnel there was an operating lever for the coal pusher. *LMS. J. B. Radford collection.*

(*right*) Rear view of tender No 9745 showing the access ladder, the tank fillers which are just visible on each side, and steam pipes and exhaust of the coal pusher. *LMS. J. B. Radford collection.*

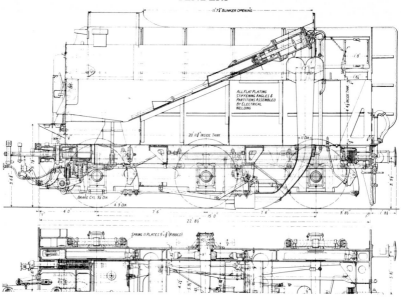

Fig 21 Coronation class streamlined tender, general arrangement. *The Railway Gazette.*

lined up with the buffer faces so that the gap between the tender and the first coach was partially closed in order to reduce wind resistance at that point. So that water column hoses could be inserted into the tank filler a door was provided through which the hose was passed. At the footplate end the tender was roofed over to match the cab roof, a bunker opening of 11ft 7¾in being left. The first five streamliners entered service without this cowling but it was soon found that it was necessary to reduce draughts. Non-streamlined locomotives of the class did not need the cowling nor rearward extension of the side sheets, although Nos 6249–52 entered service with partially streamlined tenders. The streamlined tenders also had shrouding along the bottom edge of the body to cover the springs. When streamlining was discarded all cowling, extension of side plates and spring shrouding was removed so that the tenders appeared virtually no different from those built for the non-streamlined locomotives. All tenders built for the 'Big Lizzies' had a coal pusher of the type described in the previous paragraph.

Welding the body instead of rivetting was introduced to the LMS in 1935 when a batch of outside-built tenders (for Class 5P5F 4–6–0 locomotives) was delivered. However the 10 ton replacement tenders (version (iii)) of 1936 for the 'Lizzies' were fully rivetted. Where welding was

used all watertight joints were welded for th
full length, but other joints were intermitten
welded. This helped to keep distortion to
minimum but small ridges formed on the outsi
of the plates; these were ground down to giv
smoother surface. Welding instead of rivetti
took just about one ton off the weight of a tend
The tenders built for the 'Big Lizzies' were a
welded.

The 4,000-gallon tenders were given ma
numbers to distinguish those that were rivett
from those that were of welded constructi
These marks were:

    I Rivetted 9-ton (some were partly welde
   II Welded 9-ton or 10-ton (some we
      completed with rivetted bodies includi
      the 10 tons version)
 III Rivetted 10-ton
 IV Welded 10-ton (fully-streamlined)
  V Welded 10-ton (not streamlined)

Tender and Mark numbers are detailed
Table 9.

In June 1943 instructions were issued
remove the streamline shrouding on the tend
of Nos 6220–9/35–44 and the partially-bu
tenders for Nos 6245–50 to increase coal capaci
this work was to be done by October 194
tenders being called in specially if necessary,
readiness for the resumption of throu
locomotive workings to Scotland. Even befo
the instruction to remove the streamline casi

from the locomotives was issued in December 1945 it had been decided in July 1945 to cut away the extended sides at the rear to facilitate the filling of the tank – it seems doubtful that any were done before the locomotives were de-streamlined.

The tenders built for the streamlined locomotives had two tank fillers, one each side adjacent to the doors cut into the extended side panels; access was by means of a ladder on the back of the body. For the non-streamlined locomotives the normal layout with one central tank filler and standard bracket steps on the rear of the body sufficed. There was another difference which remained after the removal of the streamlining; on those formerly streamlined the tender side panels reached a higher point at the footplate end (although the handrails were of the same length) with a consequently smaller cutaway curved section below the cab roof extension.

One other type of tender was used in traffic with a 'Big Lizzie'. Because of the absence of water troughs between Waterloo and Exeter No 46236 during the Locomotive Exchanges of 1948 had eight-wheel Ministry of Supply tender No 79294 attached to give 5,000 gallons capacity. Despite the fact that the locomotive had been renumbered and the LMS never owned such tenders, the tender was grandly lettered LMS!

Streamlined tender No 9703 (for No 6220), showing the rearward extension of the sides, with sliding upper panels for water column bag access, shrouding over the springs, but no shrouding for the coal space. *LMS, J. B. Radford collection.*

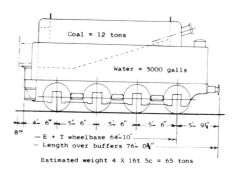

Fig 22 Proposed tender for No 6256/7, (1947). *Prepared from material supplied by Mr J. B. Radford.*

CHAPTER 8

OUT ON THE ROAD

Naturally, the directors of the LMS wanted to see what they were getting for the money spent on a brand-new design and their inspection of No 6200 was set for the end of June 1933. At Crewe Works staff strove hard to have the locomotives completed but there was so much to do and it was not until the day before that it was ready to steam off the Works yard to make its way without any previous trial running to Euston. It was at 5.00am that this giant of LMS engines was eased out of the Works and through Crewe station to run light up to London in an easy time of ten hours. Mr R. A. Riddles, then Assistant Works Superintendent, rode as far as Rugby, there handing over to Mr F. A. Lemon, the Works Superintendent, being accompanied by buckets of oil on the footplate and making many stops to feel round the bearings and add oil as required. Then as now, news of a special movement got round quickly and even as they started away from Crewe they were cheered on by railwaymen and then by others at every station and along the line! Just south of Rugby crosshead metalling ran out due to heating and the locomotive, then not named, returned to Rugby. Repairs were soon done and without a hint of the events of the previous day the 'newest lady on the line' was given full approval by the company's directors and an admiring press on 28 June.

Soon afterwards a Press run was arranged, taking place on Tuesday 15 August, the locomotive by now having its nameplates affixed. The load was 14 coaches, 560 tons, and a good start was made by not having any assistance up Camden incline. A maximum of 75mph was achieved near Leighton Buzzard but some ten miles south of Stafford trouble occurred when the left intermediate coupled axlebox ran hot. The driver had managed to get through the small cab front window onto the platform so that he could pour oil onto the axlebox, but of course it burst into flames, whereupon the train was brought to a stand. Riddles, who was travelling in the train, then decided to carry on very easily rather than await assistance and Crewe was reached 45 minutes late. It was a risk, but cautious running

had paid off. However, the affected journal was so badly scored that the axle had to be scrapped. This trip was followed by a series of clearance tests after which runs with the dynamometer car attached took place.

As soon as possible the first two locomotives were put to work on the Royal Scot express, handling the train throughout the 401 miles between Euston and Glasgow each day. Re-manning took place at Carlisle, the down train having called at Rugby and Crewe; the up train ran non-stop from Carlisle to Euston. Times were not unduly fast but gave ample opportunity for the enginemen to get to know their charge.

Firing proved onerous for many firemen, using the methods then in vogue for other locomotives, but it was quickly found that the best results were attained by firing heavily just under the firehole door and thinly towards the front, the sloping grate doing the rest. For many men it became the practice to put more and more into the firebox just ahead of the door and then add even more until the firehole was jammed solid with coal – a far cry from textbook exhortations of 'little and often'! There was an early problem for the firemen as the tender was not as self-trimming as the designers intended and so towards the end of a journey a large amount of coal had to be fetched forward. This complaint led to the first tender changes in 1935. However there was still not a good margin for the unexpected patch of bad coal, adverse weather, or operating difficulties that might occur. Unlike the Great Western Railway Kings which were always supposed to get the best (and usually did) varied coals were used, each requiring its own technique. At Camden, West Midlands or Yorkshire, both hard, would be tipped on, Crewe would supply a good quality Welsh variety and Glasgow generally provided a local soft coal, all of which could be encountered in a single trip as the fireman worked his way through the bunker. The variation in calorific value was some 2,500BTU/lb.

With the change to larger superheaters in 1935 any need to nurse the locomotives was eliminated

and in both daily performance and on special duties new records in running were set up.

An early problem was the length of the locomotive with its tender – shed collisions caused No 6201 to visit Crewe Works in April and July 1934.

In June 1935 an up run covered the 153¾ miles from Crewe to Willesden in 129½ minutes with the load being 453 tons tare, giving an average of 70¾mph. Top speed was 86½mph, achieved on the downhill stretch through King's Langley, 21 miles north of Euston. This was but a prelude to a special test run by No 6200 between Crewe and Glasgow and back with a load of 461 tons, including dynamometer car. The highlight of the tests was the covering of the 37 miles 68 chains between Lancaster and Shap summit in 41¾ minutes, speed not falling below 35mph at any point, having stopped at Lancaster. When the 1936 timetable was introduced this section was allowed 45 minutes start to pass.

On a more permanent basis the 'Lizzies' were in charge of the pre-war Merseyside Express, normally loaded to more than 500 tons, taking over from the Royal Scot 4–6–0s. This train ran non-stop from Euston to Mossley Hill 189 miles 60 chains, on the down journey, being allowed 200 minutes, and published records show that time was usually kept or slightly improved upon with ease. Dynamometer trials with No 6210 showed that performance remained high, even as the mileage approached 100,000, the actual

No 6200 The Princess Royal in its early days, having arrived at Euston in May 1934. It shows a Western Division No 1 (Camden) shedplate on the smokebox door and carries the Caledonian-style semaphore route indicator. Author's collection.

mileage at the start being 98,977 since new. With a tare load of 522 tons, the average speed between Euston and Glasgow was 52mph, coal consumption 45lb/mile (2·98lb/dbhp hr), water consumption 37·2 gallons/mile and the evaporation rate 8.3lb of water per lb of coal. This led to the acceleration of the Mid-day Scot to cover the journey from Euston to Glasgow in 7 hours 35 minutes with stops at Crewe, Lancaster, Penrith and Carlisle.

Test runs in connection with vacuum brake performance in May 1936 give an authenticated speed of 102·5mph when on the third of that month No 6203 with a load of seven coaches (total train weight 366 tons) ran between Crewe and Willesden, the maximum being reached at the 39th milepost just south of Leighton Buzzard. There have been other recorded maxima of 95–96mph.

The highlight of the career of the Princess Royal Class before their eclipse by the larger Pacifics was a test run by No 6201 down to Glasgow on 16 November 1936, returning back up the next day, having a load of 225 tons tare down and 255 up. By this time the locomotive had a domed boiler with a 32-element superheater and 119 2⅜in tubes. Preparations

Following the introduction of the Coronati
Class the older Pacifics were not entire
surpassed and they remained fully utilise
continuing to work between Euston, Glasgo
and Perth, and on Liverpool trains. They had
short spell on Euston–Manchester express
running via Crewe (being prohibited fro
passing through Stoke-on-Trent) in late 193
while they covered new ground for a while
1940 when they worked the Irish Mail servic
between Euston and Holyhead. In post-war yea
the 'Lizzies' were still to be found on Eusto
Liverpool workings, from Crewe to Euston a
to Glasgow and Perth on Anglo–Scottish trai
less frequently running right through fro
Euston to Glasgow. The Crewe to Perth diagra
were double home jobs for the men, who lodg
at Perth during the day. Their locomotives we
not idle, often being used by Perth to work
Aberdeen and back, or to a lesser extent
Glasgow Buchanan Street. They were se
seldom in Edinburgh Princes Street. Apart fro

(*left*) Hard at work tackling Shap. No 46203 *Prince*
Margaret Rose on the 11.15am down Birmingha
Glasgow express near Scout Green on 30 August 195
J. E. Wilkinson.

(*below*) Less familiar duties included milk tanks a
fish traffic. No 46201 *Princess Elizabeth* gets away fro
Perth with the up 4.45pm fish train in 1962. *W. J.*
Anderson.

for the test were very thorough and included the
fitting of a speedometer. Many miles were
covered at speeds well in excess of 80mph, hitting
or exceeding 90mph near Bletchley, Nuneaton,
Betley Road and Lockerbie on the down and just
north of Crewe, Lichfield, Rugby and Watford
coming up.

Nos 6204 and 6210 were involved about 1937
in some experimental work to determine boiler
efficiency being fitted with gas analysis
equipment under the auspices of the company's
Advisory Committee on Scientific Research.
Little has come to light on those tests, which
attempted to assess boiler efficiency for various
running conditions, such as climbing Shap. On
the Pacifics tests were run with various sizes of
superheater elements, 1⅜in double-pass, 1¼in
and 1⅛ bifurcated, and triples (size not stated
but probably 1in). Nothing much was established
but the surprise was the apparently small effect of
increasing the number of elements from 24 to 32,
No 6204 then having only a 24-element
superheater.

the overnight sleepers, up workings often included a heavily-laden up fish train originating at Aberdeen.

Other than test running the greater part of the life of the 'Turbomotive' was spent between Euston and Liverpool and a pre-war diagram frequently worked was the 10.40am down in the morning, coming back up on the 5.25pm, known unofficially as the 'Liverpool Flyer' which at that time was the fastest booking on the LMS with an average of 64·5mph between Crewe and Willesden where the train then stopped. Another diagram was 6.05pm down, the evening Merseyside Express, returning with the 10.10am up express the next day. The load of these trains was usually in excess of 500 tons and often as much as 540 tons, but they were handled with ease. No 6202 shared these jobs with other 'Lizzies'. In post-World War II days 'Turbomotive' became associated with the 8.05am down and the 5.25pm back – it was on this duty that its successor *Princess Anne* came to grief on 8 October 1952. As a turbine machine No 6202 had a reserve of power over the others in the class, illustrated by comparing rail horsepower:

	Princess Royals	Turbo-motive
Evaporation (lb/hr)	30,000	30,000
Rail hp @ 30mph	1,570	2,050
Rail hp @ 40mph	1,700	2,270
Rail hp @ 50mph	1,770	2,350
Rail hp @ 60mph	1,800	2,400
Rail hp @ 70mph	1,770	2,350

These figures illustrate that the design criteria of providing a locomotive capable of hauling the heaviest expresses on the LMS at speeds of 60mph had been achieved adequately. In its early days No 6202 worked through to Glasgow several times and proved equally capable of making 30mph on Shap and Beattock and could average 60–65mph on easier stretches. During

No 6202 in service, probably on a down train on the Trent Valley line. This view shows the long casing on the left-hand side containing the turbine steam valve control rods. The forward turbine lay on this side (casing seen in the position that would be occupied by the outside cylinders). *Real Photographs/Ian Allan.*

Because of its short working life, views of No 46202 *Princess Anne*, are rare. Only a few days out of shops the former turbine locomotive stands at Crewe on the up side at the south end of the platforms. *Real Photographs/Ian Allan.*

dynamometer trials in October 1936 No 6202 made two down and up trips in 2½ days, covering 3,200 miles. No 6210 also did this in the same series of trials. In a further series of tests which took place in 1936 and 1937 loads varied from 450 tons to 570 tons tare between Euston and Symington (where Edinburgh portions were detached or attached) and average speeds were 53–55mph, average drawbar hp ranging from 788 to 943.

Once high-speed running had been shown to be feasible the track between London and Glasgow had to be attended to so that some 50 places where speed was restricted could be eliminated or eased. In particular, curves designed for trains running at 60mph to 70mph had to be realigned for speeds up to 90mph, 75mph being considered the desirable minimum, but that was not possible everywhere. At several junctions layouts were modified so that the major route trains could pass without restriction, platforms had to be altered where curves were realigned and other loading gauge restrictions modified as much as practicable. At some places where mining subsidence caused severe reductions in speed the LMS had to buy out mining rights so that no more coal was removed from below the tracks, the section at Polesworth being the prime example. Not far away at Stafford the most extensive junction remodelling took place so that main line trains (the Trent Valley line) could traverse the junction at 55mph while Birmingham line trains were still restricted to 30mph. By careful planning previously non-existent restrictions were kept to a minimum and of the worst that had existed ten were considerably eased and six eliminated. The one place that remained heavily restricted (at 20mph for passing trains) had to wait almost fifty year before British Railways decided that it had to go Crewe! It was now possible for the LMS to introduce its high-speed Anglo-Scottish service.

No 6220 was hardly a month old when a special Press run was arranged for the 29 June 193 between Euston and Crewe. The down journey was run to the Coronation Scot timings, gaining five minutes by Stafford. Then after slowing through that station it was some distance before the locomotive was opened-out, clearing Whitmore at 85mph and then flying down the bank through Madeley and Betley Road t Crewe, accelerating past the 100mph mark to maximum of 114mph recorded by the locomotive speedometer only two miles from Crewe! A full brake application seemed at first to have no effect but then speed was steadily reduced, although the series of crossovers at the entry to No Platform was taken at 57mph, not the normal permitted 20mph, No 6220 taking the curve beautifully, unlike the crockery in the dining cars! The 'French' bogie had proved its worth The 10 miles 39 chains from Whitmore to Crew had taken no more than 6 minutes 58 second Observers on the train made the maximum spee 113mph, exactly equal to the LNER reco attained only the previous day and it will never ertain that the LMS exceeded that speed. But it was really the return journey that showed the capabilities of No 6220 which covered the 158 miles in 119 minutes exactly at an average speed of 79·7mph. Welton to Willesden, 69 miles 72 chains, was covered at an average of 87·4mph and included 100mph at Castlethorpe, 99mph at King's Langley and 96mph at Wembley, the load being 236 tons tare. The day had been one of the greatest in the history of steam in Britain.

The really great performance of the Coronation Class occurred on 26 February 1939 when No 6234, modified with a double blastpipe and chimney made the double home trip between Crewe and Glasgow, a total distance of 487 miles, with no more than two hours' turnround and no special attention to the fire. The purpose was not to test the locomotive in normal service for time and gradients but to push it to the limit on loading. This was made up to no fewer than twenty coaches, 604 tons tare, including the dynamometer car. Thus the locomotive had to lift this load unassisted from virtually sea level at Carnforth to 914ft above sea level at Shap in 31 miles 49 chains and again by 1,000ft from Carlisle to Beattock summit in 49 miles 62 chains. The first-mentioned ascent was made in 33 minutes 20 seconds at an average of 56·5mph and the second in 56 minutes 10 seconds, averaging 53·2mph, both summits being cleared at just about 30mph. Yet the finest effort was made on the up journey, taking over twice the load of the Coronation Scot from Glasgow to Carlisle in only 1½ minutes

more than the schedule of that train! The climb from Motherwell to Beattock summit, 39 miles 56 chains, is none too easy and includes many miles of about 1 in 100, or a little less steep, but the minimum up the final 1 in 99 to the summit was taken at 62mph — who in pre-electric days would ever have expected to clear Beattock at a mile a minute! It was on this ascent that the greatest drawbar pull recorded by steam in Britain occurred, being 2,282hp, equivalent to a calculated indicated horsepower of 3,333hp. Drawbar horsepowers in the range 1,800–2,000 were recorded over considerable distances; coal consumption averaged 68·7lb/mile and the 3·12lb/dbhp-hr was comparable with everyday performances. Two weeks earlier the same locomotive had been tested with the same load, but in the original single-chimney state. On that occasion it had been impossible to keep time or full steam pressure. On setting out on the second trip there must have been some among the test team who wondered if any improvement would be achieved, but any such fears were shown to be groundless.

This sort of performance was well above normal requirements in LMS day-to-day running, and unlike the LNER the former did not attempt to close the gap. There were occasions worthy of note, such as the day that No

In open country near Brinklow, No 6221 *Queen Elizabeth* hauls the down Coronation Scot on 23 September 1937. *T. G. Hepburn/Rail Archive Stephenson.*

6244 got away with 475 tons from a stand at Oxenholme South Signalbox, accelerating to 59mph at Hay Fell on a rising 1 in 131 and clearing Grayrigg at 57mph. A more usual performance, checked by the addition of a dynamometer car, was that of No 6220 on the Coronation Scot, laden to 331 tons tare, when a coal consumption of 39·2lb/mile and 3·03lb/dbhp hr was recorded; the average drawbar horsepower of the journey was 825.

When the newly formed British Railways held the Locomotive Exchange Trials in·1948, the former LMS express motive power was set against a Gresley LNER Class A4 Pacific, a GWR King 4–6–0 and a Southern Railway Merchant Navy Class 4–6–2. Perhaps surprisingly the group included another LMS class, the Converted Scot 4–6–0. No 46236 *City of Bradford* was used, and the performance was none too enterprising. In popular view the whole affair took on the air of a sporting contest, but the driver concerned thought that he would gain the

best assessment on the basis of the lowest possi coal consumption. Thus output was kept do and only once was an equivalent draw horsepower of 2,400 achieved, climbing fr Seaton Junction towards Honiton Tunnel, even that was little more than momenta However on the Western Region ascents Dainton, Rattery and Hemerdon banks w some of the best recorded. The routes wor over during the trials were Euston to Carli Paddington to Plymouth, Waterloo to Exeter King's Cross to Leeds. It was on the latter r that the 'French' bogie again showed its sup guidance — on an up journey when approach Peterborough the ex-LMS driver left reduc the speed to the permitted 20mph on the no end entry curves to the up platform almost late, coming in at close on 60mph! The ex-LN conductor driver had been far from co-opera and was not well disposed towards the drive 'another railway' — tradition dies hard, e when the forces that had brought the 'Big Fo together were enthusiastically supported railwaymen.

It was not until rather late in their history t the 'Big Lizzies' were tested at the Rugby Test Station. There in 1956 No 46225 proved that boiler could deliver continuously 40,000lb ste per hour, a drawbar horsepower of 2,250, but

No 46236 *City of Bradford* during the Locomotive Exchanges of May 1948 with Southern Region headcode as it stands ready to leave Templecombe with an up train. The tender has been taken from a War Department 2–8–0; the LMS never owned such tenders, but its was adorned with the letters LMS just to show those on 'foreign' railways just whose locomotive it was! *Real Photographs/Ian Allan.*

ring rate well beyond that possible for any but short bursts, such as that of No 6234 on its 504-ton test train. The static tests were followed by road testing between Carlisle and Skipton and the figures released afterwards showed that at 50mph the indicated horsepower reached 2,100 and drawbar horsepower 1,570, the firing rate being 3,820lb/hr. Also in 1955 No 46237 was tested on the Western Region between Paddington and Plymouth, using that Region's dynamometer car. The purpose of these tests was to make a comparison with the latest modifications to the ex-GWR King Class, the fitting of an enlarged superheater and double chimney – Swindon was just reaching the point that Stanier had got to 20 years earlier! The locomotive was handled by Western Region enginemen and inspectors. No 6013 *King Henry VIII* previously had been tested with a similar load, starting with 490 tons gross, reduced by slipping at Heywood Road Junction (near Westbury) to 420 tons. The Pacific showed its superiority at three places, in its very smart start from Reading, by not dropping below 64mph on the climb from Westbury to Brewham summit and a minimum of 46mph at Whiteball, against the King's 60mph and 37mph. The two locomotives were of virtually the same tractive effort rating, but the Pacific was capable of developing the greater horsepower. The figures based on steaming at 30,000lb/hr were:

Speed mph	Drawbar horse power	
	King	Coronation
30	1,640	1,735
50	1,540	1,765
70	1,190	1,570

Once replacement by the first generation of British Railways diesel locomotives commenced the Pacifics were displaced from regularly handling the principal trains, but there was no deterioration in performance whenever they deputised. Indeed it could hardly have been otherwise as the replacement diesels, the English Electric 2,000hp Type 4 (later Class 40) had a maximum drawbar horsepower of 1,350. Two post-World War II runs were outstanding and can be used as illustrations of peak performance. The earlier was a special run in 1953 and the second the up Caledonian express on 5 September 1957. The special run with No 46241 was laid on for a large party which had attended the opening of a new factory near Glasgow and the opportunity was taken to have a high-speed

run with a schedule of 387 minutes for the 401½-mile journey, with stops at Carlisle (to change enginemen), Crewe and Watford. With a load of eight coaches, 250 tons, and a late start of 30 minutes, the train cleared Shap in 32 minutes from Carlisle, despite being checked at Plumpton and the 50mph limit then in force at Penrith. On the level south of Carnforth a top speed of 110mph was achieved, and Lancaster to Preston cleared in 18 minutes. This effort resulted in passing Weaver Junction no more than six minutes down, but a signal failure at Crewe caused a late arrival of eleven minutes. There the dining car staff asked that things be taken more easily as they could not serve! So the running was more restrained to Lichfield, but the train was only three minutes late passing Rugby; it was unfortunate that further delays resulted in arriving at Euston seven minutes late. The driver of the up Caledonian was officially given the chance to attempt a faster than usual run from Carlisle, the locomotive being No 46244. The arrival at Euston was no less than 37 minutes early with an actual time of 253 minutes (242 net), 100mph being attained near Hindcaster Junction, Castlethorpe, King's Langley and Wembley, while Tring summit was cleared at over 90mph (but probably not the 96 mph claimed in some quarters), the estimated drawbar horsepower being 1,700 at that point. The 54 miles 42 chains from Roade to Willesden Junction were run at an average of 92mph and the times and speeds from Crewe to Euston were very close to the up run of No 6220 on 29 June 1937.

In the early part of 1956 the Western Region found that major defects were affecting the bogies of the King Class 4–6–0s, and they had to be withdrawn for immediate attention. To help out, four Stanier Pacifics were borrowed for a short while, the dates of use being:

No	To Western Region	Off Western Region	Depot
46207	1/2/1956	26/2/1956	Old Oak Common
46210	2/2/1956	18/2/1956	Old Oak Common
46254	23/1/1956	25/2/1956	Old Oak Common
46257	24/1/1956	14/2/1956	Old Oak Common

No 46237 ran on the WR from 20/4/1955 to 21/5/1955 (Bristol)

The two 'Lizzies' were first used between Paddington and Wolverhampton Low Level, but because of problems at Wolverhampton in getting the locomotives turned quickly enough, they joined the 'Biz Lizzies' on the West of England turns. One diagram was to go down on the 10.30am, the Cornish Riviera Limited, and return on the 7.15am from Plymouth the next day; other turns were the 1.30pm ex-Paddington, returning on the 8.30am from Plymouth the following morning. Workings to Bristol were included, going down on the 11.15am and 1.18pm trains, coming back up on the 1.50pm and 4.15pm afternoon departures from Bristol.

'Big Lizzies' appeared at Euston up to the end of December 1963, when No 46245 arrived with the up Royal Scot on the 28th, and No 46228 came in the next day on a parcels train. Just a few stand-in turns occurred during the early part of 1964. The last day on which the Caledonian ran was 4 September 1964 when the train was hauled by No 46238 from Crewe to Carlisle — surely that must have been arranged — about the same time No 46228 worked the down Midday Scot to Carlisle, loaded to 423 tons and covering the 141 miles 6 chains in 141½ minutes. Hopes that these magnificent locomotives would find further employment on the Southern Region between Waterloo and Bournemouth were dashed because of restricted clearances in the Southampton area.

The last working day for the eighteen still available (No 46226 lay out of use at Kingmoor with a fractured cylinder but not condemned) was Thursday 10 September and all but No 46256 were then condemned. One or two *might* have worked a day or two longer. Shortly before on 29 August No 46245 was a major exhibit at Derby Locomotive Works Open Day and the same locomotive made the last appearance of the class at a London terminus (until 1985) when it ran into Paddington on Tuesday 1 September with an Ian Allan tour. The very last working by a Stanier Pacific under British Railways ownership took place on Saturday 26 September when No 46256 headed a Railway Correspondence & Travel Society special ('The Lowlander') between Crewe and Carlisle in both directions. The load was 416 tons (450 gross) and Brock was passed at 74mph, with minimum speeds of 42mph on Grayrigg, 60mph through Tebay (after a check) and 38mph over Shap, having achieved an estimated drawbar horsepower of 2,400 at Tebay North interblock signal, taking 90½ minutes from Preston to Carlisle (90 miles 7 chains). On the up journey Shap was cleared in 38¾ minutes (31 miles 21 chains from Carlisle). This was the end and the locomotive was put into store the following Monday, being condemned on 3 October 1964. The tragedy is that *Sir William A.*

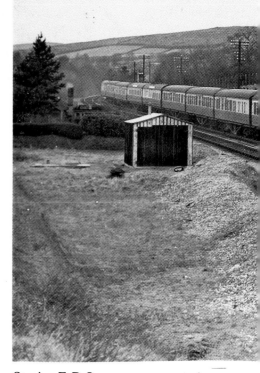

Stanier, F.R.S., was not preserved.

Accidents involving Stanier Pacifics detailed in Appendix 3 but another incident [to be mentioned here. No 6232 was ba damaged on 16 November 1940 in the vicinity Berkhamsted when a stick of Nazi bombs str the girders of Rose Lane overbridge. As th girders fell the locomotive ran into them a amazingly there were no casualties. The train v the 10.00am down from Euston.

In LMS and British Railways operat instructions it was laid down that Pacifics sho not be coupled together and when assisted t must be coupled to the train; only locomotive 4-4-0, 4-6-0 or 2-6-4T classes were permitte run coupled for assisting purposes.

To sum up, enginemen by and large w proud of the Stanier Pacifics, although firem were apt to view the huge firebox as something a penance at times, but the locomotives w rarely found wanting for steam. Drivers ha machine that gave them a good reserve in all the most adverse conditions, and both clas seemed to handle well whatever an individ driver's technique. It was perhaps fortuitous t both classes worked on the former London

Far from its home ground No 46210 *Lady Patricia*, piloted by GWR 4–6–0 No 6834 *Dummer Grange*, descends Rattery on the up Cornish Riviera on 15 February 1956. One problem of such assistance was the need to pull all the 'strings' on the coaches when the GWR locomotive was detached as it created 25in Hg vacuum compared with the 21in of the LMS locomotive. *D. S. Fish.*

North Western section of the LMS and did not need a delicate touch — former Midland men would have cringed at the sight of such massive locomotives and taken some while to get the best out of them had any been sent to work out of St Pancras when they first appeared! Firing methods reflected old LNWR practice, so it was just as well that the locomotives could take the massive filling of the firebox that was normal before starting. The fact that both drivers and firemen loved them, despite grumbles at times, is doubtless the best test that can be applied — the Stanier Pacifics were not found wanting.

One of the principal post-war trains worked by the 'Big Lizzies' was the Royal Scot between London and Glasgow. No 46240 *City of Coventry* awaits the 10.00am departure from Glasgow on 22 July 1955. *J. N. Faulkner.*

CHAPTER 9

CORONATION SCOT ON TOUR

The American railroads were extremely interested in the Coronation Scot train and during the planning of the 1939 World Fair approached the LMS with a suggestion that a complete train should not only be exhibited but should also tour the eastern part of the United States of America. Running over the tracks of eight American railroads, the tour planning was co-ordinated by the Federal Interstate Commerce Commission.

The LMS wholeheartedly agreed and prepared a set of the latest vehicles, which together with the locomotive appeared in the red and gold livery rather than the blue used initially in 1937. The train comprised:

Locomotive No 6220 *Coronation*,
Corridor brake first-class ⎫
Corridor first-class ⎪ articulated in
Corridor first-class lounge ⎬ pairs on
First-class diner ⎪ three four-
Kitchen car ⎪ wheel bogies
Third-class diner ⎭
Sleeping car — six-wheel bogies
Club saloon — four-wheel bogies

There was air-conditioning throughout, adjustable to give hot or cold air. The system had general control thermostats in the air ducting and master thermostats in each coach to regulate locally air temperature. The total tare weight was 262 tons. Although the locomotive was numbered 6220 it was No 6229 that made the journey; the exchange of numbers and names was temporary and each reverted to its original in 1942. Apart from the red livery instead of blue the giveaway to the knowledgeable observer was the air louvres in the streamlined panelling just ahead of the cylinders. The locomotive was fitted with a bell and electric headlight in order to conform to American regulations, but did not have an automatic warning system installed.

The train was placed under the care of Mr R. A. Riddles, then Mechanical & Electrical Engineer, Scotland, with Driver F. C. Bishop and Fireman J. Carswell. A foreman from Crewe Works, F. W. Soden travelled as 'master

mechanic'. Prior to leaving the United Kingdom the locomotive and train were exhibited at Euston and an official luncheon held to bid the team farewell; representatives of those who had built the locomotive and coaches were also present. Only one shipping line had vessels suitable to carry such a cargo; these were the 'Bel' ships of the Norwegian Christian–Smith Line and it was arranged to load the *Belpamela* at Southampton on 20 January 1939. A special track was laid down on the quayside and tested by a Southern Railway Lord Nelson Class 4–6–0 and the complete train was hauled dead to Southampton on 19 January 1939. The locomotive, with some parts removed, tender and one coach were stowed in the hold put there by the ship's own 150-ton derrick, and the other seven coaches travelled as deck cargo securely lashed across the beam. Southampton dockers took the opportunity of sending greetings to their opposite numbers by attaching a large inscribed sheet to one of the coaches. A late start and mountainous seas delayed arrival at Baltimore by six days. Mr Riddles and the enginemen travelled by trans-Atlantic liner and were ready to supervise the unloading and marshalling of the train prior to pulling it out of the Baltimore & Ohio Railroad shops at Mount Clare. Here final preparations were made refitting all the parts removed for the voyage so that the train was ready for its 3,120-mile tour starting with a special viewing for many distinguished persons on 17 March.

The next day a Press run was staged between Baltimore and Washington, preceeded by a special display of *Coronation* and several of the largest American express locomotives in the yard adjacent to Camden station, put on mainly for the benefit of photographers. At Washington *Coronation* stood alongside and was dwarfed by the Baltimore & Ohio locomotive *President Lincoln*. Before the return journey to Baltimore there was a staged photographic run when the Coronation Scot ran on the eastbound track and the Capital Limited on the westbound so that they crossed side-by-side the Thomas Viaduct over the Patusco River, dating from 1835 and the oldest stone railway viaduct in the world

Photographers not only photographed the trains while stationary but also on the move, being pulled ahead of them on a flat wagon. After returning to Washington for an official luncheon given by the LMS, there was yet another photographic spectacular, followed by another run of the two trains, the Capitol Limited being diesel hauled this time, to the Point of Rocks, alongside the Potomac River, making several photographic stops. After a hard and busy day the Coronation Scot returned to Baltimore. The quality of the coal supplied came as a nasty shock to both Riddles and the enginemen. In their judgement it was hardly better than slack, although adequate for use with mechanical stokers. Extra coal had to be taken at Washington during the day and it was estimated that some 11–12 tons had been used that day for no more than about 150 miles!

The host railway, the Baltimore & Ohio, had taken a great deal of care to arrange a successful tour and probably never in the history of railways the world over has a train received so much publicity, nor such hospitality. The train started from Baltimore on Tuesday 21 March at 10.00 pm precisely, setting off by a time signal initiated at the World Fair in New York. The itinerary was:

(*above*) No 6220 *Coronation* alongside a Baltimore & Ohio RR diesel locomotive at Baltimore on 18 March 1939. *Crown Copyright, courtesy National Railway Museum.*

(*below*) The substitute No 6220 *Coronation* (formerly No 6229) and train leaving Washington DC on 18 March 1939. *Crown Copyright, courtesy National Railway Museum.*

Date	Railroad	Destination
22 March	Baltimore & Ohio	Washington
23 March	Pennsylvania	Wilmington
23 March		Philadelphia
24 March		Lancaster
24 March		Harrisburg
25 March		Pittsburg
26 March	Baltimore & Ohio	Wheeling
26/27 March		Columbus
27 March	Big Four	Dayton
28 March		Cincinatti
29 March	Louisville & Nashville	Louisville
30 March		Indianapolis
30 March	Pennsylvania	Terre Haute
31 March		St Louis
1 April	Alton	Springfield (Ill)
2 April		Chicago
3 April	Michigan Central	Kalamazoo
3 April		Battle Creek
4 April		Detroit
5 April	New York Central	Toledo
5/6 April		Cleveland
6 April	Baltimore & Ohio	Akron
6 April		Kent
7 April		Youngstown
7 April	New York Central	Erie
8 April		Buffalo
9 April		Rochester
9 April		Syracuse
10 April		Utica
10 April		Schenectady
11 April		Albany
11 April	Boston & Albany	Springfield (Mass)
12 April		Worcester
12/13 April		Boston
13 April	New York, New Haven &	Providence
14 April	Hartford	Hartford
14 April		New Haven

The train came to rest at the Fairground in New York City at 11.00pm on 14 April. The dates given are the days on which the train was open to public viewing.

The running between successive stops was usually only about two to three hours, but the stretch from Harrisburg to Pittsburg took 6½ hours. For a morning stop the train normally arrived a little before midnight, and then moved on in the early afternoon to a second stop, remaining there until between 9.00pm and 10.00pm. Only the major centres of Pittsburg, Columbus, Cincinatti, Louisville, St Louis, Chicago, Detroit, Cleveland, Buffalo and Boston had a full day, a few being the afternoon of arrival and the following morning. In contrast the stop at Kent was intended to be of no more than one hour, this town being the home of Charles C. Green, the Director of Promotion of the World Fair, travelling with the train and using the first-class dining car as an exhibition coach. Even there up to 3,000 persons were awaiting the train's arrival. Everywhere the train was met by vast crowds with bands and all the noise that Americans love to have on festive occasions, but Mr Riddles always took care to ask the local mayor to open the exhibition.

Mechanically the train behaved well, but there were two major items needing attention. The first was the renewal of the locomotive firebox brick arch at Harrisburg. The replacement failed due to poor fitting and the arch was replaced again at St Louis — Riddles himself entered the firebox while there was still plenty of steam pressure and with the help of the local boilermaker dismantled the defective arch during the early hours. After going to a hotel for less than three hours' sleep and then attending the exhibition, he spent the afternoon rebuilding the arch. There was still 50lb/sq in steam pressure in the boiler but all was ready at 5.00pm for the 9.00pm departure. In the coaches the air-conditioning master controllers had to be cut out, having possibly been damaged on the sea crossing. Otherwise matters requiring attention were less drastic, although the replacement of a broken carriage spring bolt required the turning of a suitable piece of steel to produce it. In contrast the elimination of a mysterious banging below the sleeping car, once identified, required less than fifteen minutes to adjust the spring, much to the amazement of the American fitters who were used to solid unadjustable links.

Not only was Mr Riddles responsible for the train throughout the tour but he also had to drive for much of the way as Driver Bishop had caught pneumonia and did not drive until 9 April. Riddles took his share of firing, more particularly at the beginning of the tour. One unexpected aspect of driving was that it took some while for Carswell, the fireman, when driving on the first run to realise that white was used for clear signals, the conductor driver calling out their aspects. Despite the fact that the train had the capability of running at 100mph it was limited to 85mph while in the USA. Possibly the fact that it was vacuum-braked and not air-braked was behind this decision.

The tour was a great success and rather more than two million persons inspected the train on tour and at the Fair. Coronation, arrived back at Cardiff on 16 February 1942, the wartime need for motive power being so great that it was worth risking the sea voyage, but it was 1946 before the coaches could return. After the American Tour the chime whistle which had been fitted to the locomotive was installed at Crewe Locomotive Works.

CHAPTER 10

PERFORMANCE

Locomotive performance is all too frequently recorded from the narrow viewpoint of a handful of selected outstanding runs, usually not typical of everyday working and more often than not the consequence of regaining lost time, or of a special working. The subject is something much wider and in reality it is the ability to do the work required day in, day out, with the minimum of disruption from mechanical or other causes, that management regarded as 'performance'. The timetable set the target in terms of the number of trains to be run which determined the diagrams for locomotives and men and consequently the number of each required, and loads and speeds which governed the class of locomotive to be used. Against this, allowance had to be made for maintenance requirements as determined by mechanical engineering staff and ideally in British practice an availability of 85% was demanded, *ie* about eight locomotives for seven jobs. That such a figure was not at all attainable by larger passenger locomotives such as the LMS Pacifics was the consequence of various factors. Management spent appreciable time on both day-to-day causes as well as seeking long-term solutions to identifiable problems.

Locomotive availability figures in steam days were calculated from returns submitted by sheds which accounted for each locomotive day, be it used, available but not used, stopped for examinations or repairs, awaiting material, awaiting a decision on works repairs or in works. Sundays were not taken into account, although annual mileage, coal consumption, and other factors, did include that day! On this basis Table 10 shows the variations in availability on an annual basis for the years 1950 to 1958. The higher mileages of the Coronation Class on the LMR arose from the duties allotted, but for those in Scotland the mileage was disappointingly lower. It was doubtless the consequence of having less scope for locomotives based in Glasgow and working on regional-prepared diagrams, although the greater part of their mileage was run in England. It is noticeable that the mileage of the Princess Royals is much closer for the two regions. If only inter-regional running had been encouraged in those days so that traditional locomotive change points were abolished then Crewe North locomotives could have worked North-to-West trains well into the Western Region instead of handing over at Shrewsbury. The Newton Abbot–Shrewsbury double home job, worked by ex-GWR Castles would have greatly enhanced the annual mileage and some of the Cardiff or Bristol trains could have been added, no doubt turn and turn about with Kings and Castles.

TABLE 10

AVERAGE ANNUAL MILEAGE AND AVAILABILITY

Year	London Midland Region				Scottish Region			
	Princess Royal		Coronation		Princess Royal		Coronation	
	Mileage	%	Mileage	%	Mileage	%	Mileage	%
1937	74,992	57¾	-	-	-	-	-	-
1950	49,081	54	68,960	66	-	-	56,866	67¾
1951	49,725	57	67,624	69¾	51,438	60	67,617	68
1952	55,322	58	71,524	68	51,511	53½	54,031	64½
1953	58,379	59	69,464	63½	-	-	55,932	67
1954	56,337	63	73,849	68½	-	-	55,175	72
1955	56,814	62	71,284	68½	-	-	48,870	64
1956	56,444	61	74,597	64½	-	-	53,825	69
1957	56,518	63	73,159	71	-	-	49,912	69
1958	52,234	58	72,131	69	54,086	56	54,715	68

Mileage represents average per annum per locomotive.

% represents average availability of locomotives allocated.

The 1937 figure refers to the LMS.

TABLE 11

COMPARISON OF MILEAGE AND AVAILABILITY OF MAJOR PASSENGER CLASSES ON BRITISH RAILWAYS

Class	Power class	1950 miles≠	%	1954 miles≠	%	1957 miles≠	%
4-6-2 A4	8P	56,641	69	62,841	70	65,575	72
4-6-2 MN	8P	45,833	56	46,128	57	58,575	64
4-6-0 King	8P	52,978	61	51,010	56	50,328	55
4-6-2 Coronation	8P	69,649	70	74,333	72	74,144	72
4-6-2 71000	8P	-	-	-	-	37,426	55
4-6-0 Castle	7P	46,660	70	48,972	72	45,553	66
2-6-2 V2	6	39,475	75	41,233	75	43,124	77
4-6-0 Lord Nelson	7P	43,582	63	41,915	73	36,568	79
4-6-0 Royal Scot	7P	61,840	73	60,599	72	56,553	73
4-6-2 70000 LMR	7	-	-	55,395	72	58,594	65
4-6-2 70000 ER	7	-	-	74,578	75	61,232	76
4-6-2 70000 WR	7	-	-	48,266	57	45,581	63

≠ Average mileage per annum per locomotive.

Protagonists of other major express classes on British Railways will no doubt be disappointed to see from Table 11 that the LMS locomotives just managed to attain better figures than the ex-LNER A4 Class (apart from being equalled in 1957) but had greater mileages than their East Coast rivals. Neither the ex-SR Merchant Navy Class nor the ex-GWR King Class achieved the mileage or availability, both classes handicapped by not having the opportunity for runs as long as those possible on the West and East Coast routes.

It should be added that the British Railways design of Class 8P locomotive, No 71000, did not achieve either the mileage or availability of the 'Big Lizzies', being partly handicapped by its status of a solitary example. The same table also shows the performance of the next lower power group of express locomotives and to some extent shows that lower annual mileages enhance availability, although geography and operating practice, particularly the mixed-traffic use of the ex-LNER V2 Class, were sometimes adverse factors.

To illustrate the effect of maintenance requirements on performance, a brief description is given of the maintenance schedules. Broadly, running shed examinations fell into two categories, those based on wear and tear of moving parts and therefore determined mainly by mileage, and those affected by the number of days in steam, it being necessary to marry the two together when planning stoppages to meet the schedule.

Each passenger locomotive had to be examined daily and each week the major express locomotives had to be stopped at 6–8 days for a 'Boiler Full X Examination (BFX)' which comprised essentially an examination in steam, followed by a check of various items such as cylinder cocks, sanding gear, water pick-up, tender coal-pusher, self-cleaning smokebox, rocking grate and hopper ashpan to ensure that they were working freely. The boiler had to be cooled for the firebox to be examined and this was done by passing water through the boiler at a prescribed rate to displace gradually the hot water (5 gallons per minute for two hours, 12 gallons per minute for another two hours and finally 25 gallons per minute for 30 minutes). Also the tubes were to be checked for freedom from obstruction. Every fortnight (12–16 days) the boiler was washed out and had to be cooled (because the LMS used cold water for this job), like the X Examination, except that the final 25 gallons per minute had to be used for another 90 minutes so that the boiler was totally cold. For the washing out all wash-out plugs and mudhole doors had to be removed and then by using a jet of water the wash-out man cleared first the firebox crown, then the barrel (working from the tubeplate end) and finally all round the firebox water spaces, using rods where necessary. Afterwards a boilersmith thoroughly examined all parts of the boiler. Thus even the smallest

examination was prolonged not only by t cooling-down process but also lighting-up a generating steam, which on the Pacifics to upwards of six to eight hours.

Many non-moving parts had to be examined 3–5 weeks, particularly to ensure that wat gauge frame cocks and passages were clear and new gauge glasses, test the brakes (whi included an efficiency test of the ejectors) a check the train steam heating, testing t reducing valve and changing defective hoses. 7–9 weeks further work entailed the changing firebox fusible plugs, checking injectors a clacks and driver's brake valve, while at 9– weeks safety-valves were examined and check to ensure that they 'blew off' 245lb/sq in 255lb/sq in.

Moving parts were examined at intervals 5,000 to 6,000 miles, although for the LM Pacifics only wheels and tyres, and the conditi of tender tanks had to be checked this often. every 10,000 to 12,000 miles motion had to examined and partially dismantled, crank ax checked, bogies examined in position, pist rings changed, drawgear checked and axleb pads and lubrication checked. Then at 20,000 24,000 miles piston valve rings had to changed. At 30,000 to 36,000 miles t locomotive and tender had to be parted f examination of the intermediate drawgear a rubbing plates, pistons and piston valv withdrawn and checked, steam and exhaust po cleaned, smokebox fittings checked a crankpins examined. For the Pacifics it was requirement that the motion and valve gear w sent to Crewe Works for attention at th examination, so all the LMS Pacifics irrespecti of their home depots normally went to Crew North shed for this examination.

The work content of these examinations w cumulative so that the 10,000 to 12,000 mil included the 5,000 to 6,000, and so on. Somewh hopefully the motive power officer expressed tl wish that none of these examinations, exce when boiler repairs arose, would keep locomotive out of service for more than 24 hour It was fair enough for the lesser examinations, b repair work was sometimes quite substantial the major examinations. That was partly becau examination of components revealed defects a partly the extra work arising from 'deferre repairs which had been found betwe examinations but which could be left until examination was due, unless they affected the safe working of the locomotive.

No 6202 the 'Turbomotive', had its own special maintenance requirements at sheds. Each day water had to be drawn off the lubricating oil tank, oil levels checked and oil pumps tested for supply rate and pressure before the auxiliary oil pumps were started. Following each run a fitter was required to stop the auxiliary oil pumps after the locomotive had been standing for 30 minutes and check the forward turbine thrust indicator. At each BFX oil strainers were to be cleaned and control gear oiled and greased. At 5,000 to 6,000 miles oil was drained off, the oil system cleaned and fresh oil provided, feedwater heater tubes cleaned and the turbine blades and bearings checked. The roller-bearing axleboxes were checked and refilled with oil as necessary.

Numerous components became defective to some extent and could be rectified without too much difficulty at sheds, but sometimes it was beyond a shed's ability to remedy major defects, particularly those affecting the boiler or occasionally wheels and motion. One of the most unpleasant repairs that occurred all too frequently was spring replacement. Despite their simplicity, and high standard of manufacture and repair, the life of springs under the LMS Pacifics was no more on average than about seven months for bogies and trailing wheels, and nine months for coupled wheels — tender springs lasted much better, about 2½ years. On the face of it springs were rarely stressed to anywhere near the design limit, let alone safety limits and yet individual plates fractured. It was necessary to place a jack under the locomotive frame and lift far enough to take the weight off the faulty spring. Then hopefully the retaining nuts would be free enough to be moved — otherwise it meant splitting them off – on the spring hanger – and that the carrying pin would be knocked out of the spring bracket below the axlebox before letting the spring drop into the pit. Then the replacement had to be hoisted into place. Rarely, if ever, was the instruction to change the opposite spring carried out! Just now and then a locomotive would be weighed after a spring change, when almost inevitably the loads on the axles were found to be anything but the amounts specified, such was the effect of constantly changing spring loadings and stiffness from weathering and dirt affecting threads, nuts and spring pads! A special instruction was the requirement to turn the bogies of the Pacifics to even out tyre wear; as this involved lifting at sheds, the practice developed of leaving the bogie frame in position, dropping each wheelset and then changing them over.

In addition to all the shed examinations, locomotives were taken out of service for workshop overhauls and repairs, both routine and unplanned. The LMS Pacifics were proposed for shops every eight months and unless in a suitable condition for a further short period in service they entered Crewe Works for a classified repair, the categories being 'Heavy' or 'Light', dependent on the nature of the work done:

(a) boiler change made any overhaul a 'Heavy'
(b) combination of new tyres, or new cylinders or boiler retubed, or motion or brake gear overhauled would constitute a 'Heavy'
(c) 'Light' overhaul could include one of (b) and a variety of other repair jobs

Apart from the classification of 'Heavy' or 'Light' a repair was either an 'Intermediate' or 'General'. The distinction between the two was usually that the boiler remained in place for an 'Intermediate', although other work might make it a 'Heavy Intermediate'. Furthermore, the intervals between 'Intermediate' and 'General' repairs, despite the nominal eight months were not equal, especially in terms of miles, being roughly a 55/45 proportion. This was because items which did not require attention at an 'Intermediate', especially on the boiler, tended to dictate the need for the next repair.

Thus for a major passenger class the fact that higher mileages were run meant more frequent (in terms of the calendar) stoppages for examinations and workshop overhauls; therefore a lower availability was inevitable. A humble shunting or local goods engine achieved only a quarter or one-third of the mileage, although perhaps in steam for as many hours per day, needed fewer mileage examinations per annum, had fewer repairs due to wear and tear or vibration, and visits to the shops only every two or three years. The abundance of these lesser category locomotives hid the statistical shortcomings of express passenger classes, for overall LMS locomotives were achieving the desired 85%. Only when a detailed survey looked more deeply into the performance of the Pacifics was the real performance revealed and understood by 'upstairs' management.

As soon as possible after the end of World War II the Chief Mechanical Engineer undertook a detailed survey of the daily performance of both classes and then analysed examinations, repairs and defects. Availability in 1946 was 63 per cent for the English-based locomotives and only 55 per cent in Scotland. It was found that each locomotive had been into the shops twice in 1945, once for a classified repair, the other for any number of defects and collisions, and that the time out of service was excessive. The annual mileage was about 70,000 but the operating officer had based his timetables and diagrams on 83,000 miles on the assumption that the Pacifics could achieve 75 percent availability. The time at which the survey was conducted was not when locomotives were at their best, effects of six long years of war and the immediate post-war imposition of prolonged austerity by a singularly incompetent government hampering efforts to remedy the consequences of deferred maintenance and lower quality materials obtaining in those years.

There was the hope that eventually pre-war standards would be restored and overcome some of the deficiencies, but design was also studied

and it was felt that valve gear, axlebox clearanc and spring gear in particular could be improv and that advantage could be taken of wartir experiences with the American 2–8 locomotives which had drop-grates and se cleaning smokeboxes. Another wartir innovation derived from American practice w the introduction of manganese-steel liners f coupled axleboxes and roller bearings. So apa from the drive to improve matters at sheds an works, using the energies of mechanic inspectors and maintenance staff, a design targ was drawn up aimed at eliminating t weaknesses revealed, and the result was t modification of the 1937 design so that the la two locomotives of the five authorised in 19 appeared in substantially modified form, described in Chapter 5. Unfortunately separate statistical records exist to compare t performance of these two locomotives with t remainder of the 'Big Lizzies', but the whole cla improved steadily so that by 1957 mileages we 96,650 in seventeen months for an 'Intermedia repair and a further 91,671 in sixteen months f a 'General'. So the target of 100,000 miles p shopping set in 1946 was in sight, b improvement in utilisation so that such a milea could be run in twelve months just nev occurred. Once diesel and electric traction was order for West Coast main line services t emphasis changed and no further improveme was sought.

No 46235 *City of Birmingham* gets away from Aberdeen with the 3.30pm up Postal past Ferryhill Junction on 24 June 1955. *J. N. Faulkner.*

ALLOCATIONS

Initially Nos 6200/1 were sent to Camden but No 6201 was almost immediately moved to Polmadie. Then No 6200 was transferred to Kingmoor from where it worked a daily return trip to Euston, just 600 miles, and probably more than any previous daily roster in Britain. The 'Turbomotive' spent its entire working life at Camden, and so did its short-lived replacement; the transfer to Crewe North in June 1953 was a paper move only as the locomotive had been derelict since the previous October. Of the 1935-built 'Lizzies' the first two were sent to Polmadie and the rest to Camden, home for many of them in pre-World War II days, exceptions being No 6205 at Polmadie in 1935 for a few weeks and again in 1939 when several were at Edge Hill and some at Crewe North. For a while

in the autumn of 1939 Nos 6201/6–9 were stationed at Longsight, handling Manchester–Euston trains, but soon afterwards they returned to Anglo-Scottish trains, their usefulness at Manchester being limited by the fact that they were not cleared to run through Stoke-on-Trent. No 6207 had spent just a few weeks at Rugby before its move to Longsight. A most unusual location for the class was Holyhead where Nos 6203–5 were stationed for a while in 1940 for use on the Irish Mail services.

At Nationalisation all except No 6202 were allocated to Crewe North, Nos 6200/3/5 having moved from Edge Hill during 1947. Soon afterwards they began to move away from Crewe North so that in early 1950 Edge Hill had Nos 46200/1/3/5, but the most interesting move at that time was the return of the class to Polmadie, where Nos 46200/3 were sent in September 1951, their intended duties being the Birmingham–Glasgow through trains (one leaving each place just before mid-day, the other overnight) north of Crewe; however both left Glasgow in May 1953. Polmadie was again to have two more of the class when Nos 46201/10 were moved there in June 1958 but they left for Kingmoor in March 1961. Two other depots which acquired some of the class in their latter days were Carnforth (Nos 46200/3/11) and Rugby (No 46206) for a few months in 1961. At the London end of the line Camden surrendered two, Nos 46205/7 to Willesden in September 1961, but Nos 46206/9 were condemned from Camden. Table 12 gives the allocation of the class at selected dates.

Not surprisingly the Coronation locomotives were originally based at Camden, Nos 6220–48 being sent there when completed. Polmadie received its first early in the war years when Nos 6220–4/30–2 were transferred and all but Nos 6220/1 remained there until condemned. For many years the class was spread over Camden, Crewe North, Upperby and Polmadie, no other LMS shed having any, Crewe North gaining its first in 1943 and Upperby in 1946. Edge Hill had a few of the class for short intervals in post-Nationalisation days, mostly only about a month, the longest stayer being No 46251 which was

TABLE 12
LOCOMOTIVE ALLOCATIONS

Loco No	First shed	April 1944	January 1948	January 1954	June 1958	Last shed
6200	Camden	Crewe N	Crewe N	Edge Hill	Edge Hill	Kingmoor
6201	Camden	Crewe N	Crewe N	Crewe N	Polmadie	Upperby
6202	Camden	Camden	Camden	Crewe N‡	-	Crewe N‡
6203	Polmadie	Crewe N	Crewe N	Crewe N	Crewe N	Kingmoor
6204	Polmadie	Crewe N	Crewe N	Edge Hill	Edge Hill	Edge Hill
6205	Camden	Crewe N	Crewe N	Edge Hill	Crewe N	Willesden
6206	Camden	Crewe N	Crewe N	Crewe N	Crewe N	Camden
6207	Camden	Crewe N	Crewe N	Edge Hill	Edge Hill	Willesden
6208	Camden	Crewe N	Crewe N	Edge Hill	Edge Hill	Edge Hill
6209	Camden	Crewe N	Crewe N	Crewe N	Crewe N	Camden
6210	Camden	Crewe N	Crewe N	Crewe N	Polmadie	Kingmoor
6211	Camden	Crewe N	Crewe N	Crewe N	Crewe N	Crewe N
6212	Camden	Crewe N	Crewe N	Crewe N	Crewe N	Crewe N
6220	Camden	Polmadie	Polmadie	Polmadie	Crewe N	Upperby
6221	Camden	Polmadie	Polmadie	Polmadie	Crewe N	Upperby
6222	Camden	Polmadie	Polmadie	Polmadie	Polmadie	Polmadie
6223	Camden	Polmadie	Polmadie	Polmadie	Polmadie	Polmadie
6224	Camden	Polmadie	Polmadie	Polmadie	Polmadie	Polmadie
6225	Camden	Camden	Camden	Crewe N	Crewe N	Upperby
6226	Camden	Camden	Upperby	Upperby	Upperby	Kingmoor
6227	Camden	Camden	Crewe N	Polmadie	Polmadie	Polmadie
6228	Camden	Camden	Upperby	Upperby	Crewe N	Crewe N
6229	Camden	Camden	Crewe N	Camden	Camden	Edge Hill
6230	Camden	Polmadie	Polmadie	Polmadie	Polmadie	Polmadie
6231	Camden	Polmadie	Polmadie	Polmadie	Polmadie	Polmadie
6232	Camden	Polmadie	Polmadie	Polmadie	Polmadie	Polmadie
6233	Camden	Camden	Crewe N	Crewe N	Upperby	Edge Hill
6234	Camden	Crewe N	Crewe N	Crewe N	Crewe N	Upperby
6235	Camden	Camden	Crewe N	Crewe N	Crewe N	Crewe N
6236	Camden	Camden	Crewe N	Camden	Upperby	Kingmoor
6237	Camden	Camden	Camden	Camden	Upperby	Upperby
6238	Camden	Camden	Upperby	Upperby	Upperby	Upperby
6239	Camden	Camden	Camden	Camden	Camden	Crewe N
6240	Camden	Camden	Camden	Camden	Camden	Crewe N
6241	Camden	Camden	Camden	Camden	Camden	Edge Hill
6242	Camden	Camden	Polmadie	Crewe N	Camden	Polmadie
6243	Camden	Camden	Camden	Crewe N	Camden	Edge Hill
6244	Camden	Camden	Camden	Camden	Upperby	Kingmoor
6245	Camden	Camden	Camden	Camden	Camden	Crewe N
6246	Camden	Camden	Camden	Crewe N	Crewe N	Camden
6247	Camden	Camden	Camden	Camden	Camden	Kingmoor
6248	Camden	Camden	Camden	Crewe N	Crewe N	Crewe N
6249	Polmadie	-	Upperby	Camden	Crewe N	Polmadie
6250	Polmadie	-	Upperby	Camden	Upperby	Upperby
6251	Polmadie	-	Upperby	Upperby	Crewe N	Crewe N
6252	Crewe N	-	Crewe N	Crewe N	Crewe N	Camden
6253	Camden	-	Camden	Crewe N	Crewe N	Crewe N
6254	Camden	-	Camden	Camden	Camden	Crewe N
6255	Camden	-	Camden	Upperby	Upperby	Kingmoor
6256	Crewe N	-	Crewe N	Camden	Camden	Crewe N
6257	Camden	-	-	Camden	Camden	Kingmoor

* ‡ Nominal allocation (after destruction in Harrow collision).
Camden and Willesden were London sheds; Edge Hill was in Liverpool;
Upperby and Kingmoor were in Carlisle; Polmadie was in Glasgow.
Crewe N = Crewe North shed.

there in March–April 1954, September 1954 to April 1955, then May 1955 only, followed by a spell from September 1955 to May 1956. Others at Edge Hill were Nos 46226 (1953 and 1955), 46228 (1954), 46236 (1961) and 46254 (1955), but No 46233 was there from September 1960, joined by Nos 46229/41/3 in March 1961, all staying until condemned. Kingmoor acquired No 46236 in October 1960, followed by Nos 46221/6/37/44/52/5/7 in March 1961 and No 46247 in June 1961, all staying until condemned, except Nos 46221/37 which left in April 1962 and No 46252 which left in September 1962. In September 1962 Nos 46231/2 were put into store

at Carstairs and never ran again, followed by fo at the London end, Nos 46239/40/6/52 Camden. Nos 46239/40 worked again; in Augu 1963 the former was transferred (on paper onl to Holyhead, but in the next month it joined t latter at Willesden. That depot also acquired N 46245 from Camden when that shed closed steam on 9 September 1963. However these thr locomotives moved to Crewe North in Jul August 1964. Table 12 includes the allocation this class at selected dates.

The short period of the loan of four to t Western Region has been mentioned in Chapt 8, all four working from Old Oak Common she

---

APPENDIX 2

PROPOSED LARGE PASSENGER LOCOMOTIVE

The proposal to build two 'Super Pacifics' on the 1940 Locomotive Programme and their subsequent cancellation has been mentioned in Chapter 2. The objective was an improvement in thermal efficiency and enhanced power so that new ideas were concentrated on an increase in boiler pressure to 300 lb/sq in, higher degree of superheating, better steam flow through ports and passages, steel firebox with thermic syphons and arch tubes, and four cylinders 15in diameter by 28in stroke. For the exhaust a Kylchap double blastpipe was intended. In other respects and in appearance they would have been 'Big Lizzies'.

Slightly earlier in concept but only by a year, was the proposal for a much larger version of the Coronation Class. By 1938 it was clear that internal air services could become competitive between London and Glasgow, so that existing trains would have to be accelerated to do the journey in the even six hours, or a little better. Trains of 600 tons rather the 300 tons then being run were also thought to be necessary. That would have required a much larger tractive effort at higher speeds than possible with the existing Pacifics, but adhesion was not in question so a six-coupled arrangement could be retained. To burn the fuel consumed, some 10½ tons, the grate had to be larger, in fact 70sq ft, for a combustion rate of 50lb sq ft/hr, which made a

mechanical stoker a necessity as such a firing ra would have been beyond any fireman's capabili throughout the journey. This of course meant trailing bogie, so making a 4–6–4. In order produce a tractive effort a third greater at 60m the cylinders would have been 17½in diamet by 28in stroke and the boiler pressure 300lb/s in. To limit the starting tractive effort, 56,000 nominally, the maximum cut-off would hav been 65 percent, so giving 42,800lb.

For the demand stated a much bigger boil was needed and this meant that the couple wheels had to be no more than 6ft 6in diamete Then a boiler of maximum diameter 6ft 10⅜ could be fitted; interestingly the combustic chamber of the Pacific boilers was to b discarded. Tubes would have been 20ft 6in lon giving a just acceptable free gas area of 14%, th firebox being 10ft 0in long by 8ft 6in wid externally. Streamlining to save a few hundre horsepower was to be retained and a locomotiv weight of 119 tons was estimated, the maximur axle loading being 24 tons. It was anticipated tha the civil engineer would accept this due to th absence of hammerblow and the running of th 'Turbomotive' with 23 tons.

To carry sufficient coal and water a massiv 68-ton eight-wheel tender was planned, holdin 12 tons of coal and 5,000 gallons of water.

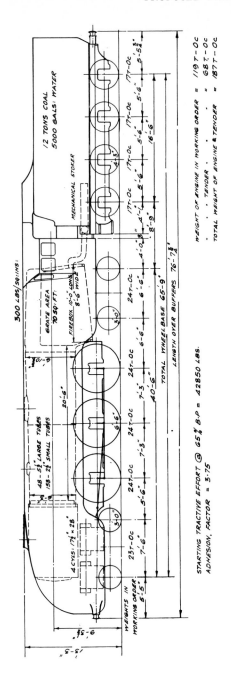

Fig 23 Proposed LMS streamlined 4–6–4 express passenger locomotive, 1938. *LMS*.

Euston to Glasgow run would have consumed some 20,000 gallons of water!

Critical was the design and capacity of the ashpan which would have to contain the ash of some 10–12 tons of coal. It may also have been found that coal consumption would have been greater (so that an even larger tender would be needed) because of the loss of the finer particles drawn straight through the tubes and out of the chimney unburnt, a fact of mechanical stoker operation not then appreciated in Britain. In view of the limited route requirement, ashpan design could have been made easier by arranging that crossovers and motive power depot shed sidings at the few places that these locomotives would have used were replaced by less sharp curvature so reducing the throw-over and giving more space in the critical area below the firebox.

The project had all the airs of reality and success had it been possible to proceed with the building of such locomotives as shown in the outline drawing. As a matter of conjecture their overall availability could well have been 70 percent despite the higher annual mileages envisaged. To work some four or five daytime high-speed trains (and no doubt sleeping car trains at night to achieve better utilisation) the company would have needed at least seven locomotives. If more trains were anticipated than were provided in 1938 then ten would have been needed and if Liverpool and Manchester were later considered then no doubt fifteen might have been expected. Even as late as December 1942 the design was still regarded as the high-speed express locomotive for the future.

ACCIDENTS

For a total mileage accumulated by the Stanier Pacifics of somewhat more than 70,000,000, and the number of trains worked, the two classes did not have a large number of accidents, but regrettably the record was marred by two firebox crown collapses. The first of these was an early wartime event when during the morning of 10 September 1940 while working the 10.00am Glasgow to Euston train a pair of inexperienced enginemen had the misfortune to allow the firebox crown to become uncovered with dire results, the fireman succumbing to his injuries. The passed fireman and the passed cleaner joined No 6224 at Glasgow Central only three minutes before departure was due and both were quite unused to so large a locomotive. The disaster occurred on the climb up to Craigenhall, between Cleghorn and Carstairs. By an amazing and unfortunate coincidence the same locomotive was involved in the second case, no more than a dozen miles away at Lamington, when working the 9.25pm Glasgow to Euston on 7 March 1948. This time the driver, well experienced with the class, lost his life, but the cause was found to be defective water gauges.

One other incident can be put down to a mechanical defect. On 21 October 1951 No 6207 while working the 8.20am up Liverpool express became derailed at Weedon at about 11.15am. Examination of the bogie immediately revealed the cause and left everyone wondering how the train had got so far that morning. The journey was the first trip after attention to the bogie two days before at Edge Hill shed. The wheelsets had been changed over to deal with a sharpening left leading flange — what had not been checked was the clearances in the axleboxes, one box in its new position being so tight that it had no vertical freedom (and the inspecting officer thought that sufficient heat had been generated during running to expand the box so that it seized). The requirement to turn bogies has been mentioned in Chapter 10. The locomotive was weighed at Crewe Works on 6 November 1951, the report quoting the following:

Wheelset	Left-hand		Right-hand	
	tons	cwt	tons	cwt
Leading bogie	5	1	4	15
Trailing bogie	5	1	4	15
Leading coupled	10	10	10	7
Driving coupled	11	6½	11	6
Trailing coupled	12	0	12	0
Rear truck	9	6	7	11½
TOTALS	53	4½	50	14½

What is not clear from the report is whether t[he] locomotive was weighed in 'working order' [or] empty – the inference is the latter, so making [a] full weight of about 110 tons.

No other accidents involving Stanier Pacif[ics] had any element of mechanical failure abo[ut] them. Two were mainly the result of tra[ck] deficiencies during and just after World War [II]. The first occurred on 1 May 1944 at Mossban[d] north of Carlisle, three passengers being kille[d]. No 6225 was hauling the 8.40pm down slee[per] (provided principally for servicemen). T[he] second was on 21 July 1947 when No 62[--] working the 8.30am down Liverpool left t[he] track at a point known as Grendon, betwe[en] Atherstone and Polesworth, while running [at] fairly high speed, five passengers losing their liv[es] (the author as a twelve-year-old was taken th[at] evening to watch the rerailing operations, stayi[ng] until well after midnight). It was recorded th[at] the track was near the end of its life and due [for] renewal in 1948, the immediate cause being [the] deterioration of gauge on a curve.

The remaining four accidents involved signa[ls,] three passed at danger, the other a signalma[n's] error. The first case was on 21 July 1945, No 62[--] being the locomotive of the 1.00 pm up Glasgo[w.] At Ecclefechan signals were ignored and the tra[in] ran into a goods which was being shunted. Bo[th] enginemen were killed, but no passenge[rs] despite heavy damage to the stock. The next w[as] on 18 May 1947 when the driver of No 62[--] heading the 1.00pm Glasgow to Euston train r[an] through signals instead of stopping at Lambri[gg] Box, near Grayrigg, where the train should ha[ve] reversed onto the down line, because the up li[ne] was blocked for repairs. Instead of stopping t[he] train collided with a light engine; amazingly [no] serious results followed, for the collisi[on] occurred on the high Docker Viaduct.

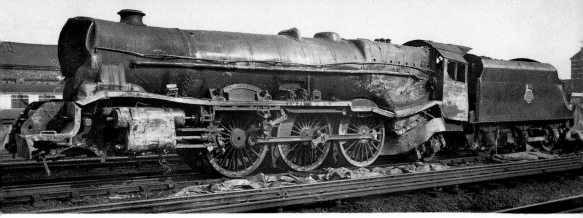

More serious than any before in terms of casualties, the collision at Winsford at 12.17am on 17 April 1948 claimed immediately the lives of 8 and a further six later. The previous day's 5.40 pm passenger from Glasgow with No 6207 and 520 tons was standing just north of Winsford Station, the communication cord having been pulled by a young soldier who aimed to shorten his homeward journey rather than go on to the next booked stop at Crewe. No 6251 was following on the up Postal (625 tons) and the train was irregularly admitted into the section because the signalman at Winsford Station Box cleared his block instruments although he had not seen the passenger train pass.

The worst railway accident in England and since the formation of British Railways, and exceeded only by the holocaust at Quintinshill on the Caledonian in 1915, involved two Stanier Pacifics. Again it was a case of passing signals at danger, the up Perth sleeper of 7 October 1952 running into an up local bound for Euston and standing at Harrow & Wealdstone at about 8.19am. This collision, with No 46242 on the sleeper, was serious enough, but before anyone

(above and below) The two wrecked Pacifics before removal to Crewe Works after the double collision at Harrow & Wealdstone on 8 October 1952. No 46202 *Princess Anne* never ran again but No 46242 *City of Glasgow* was repaired. *British Rail, R. T. Ellis collection.*

could take action to stop it and within seconds the wreckage was run into by the 8.00am down Liverpool train headed by Class 6P No 45637 and the new *Princess Anne*, the horrendous death toll reaching 112. The reason for the failure to respond to signals by the up sleeper's driver could not be established, but the autumn mist must have been a major factor. The lasting consequence was the introduction of the British Railways Automatic Warning System (then known as Automatic Train Control). Development had already reached an advanced stage (critics at the time alleging too slowly and without enthusiasm) and only nine days later the press was shown the locomotive fittings on an Eastern Region A4 Pacific preparatory to running trials between Barnet and Huntington on the East Coast Main Line. Harrow gave the impetus to finalise design, accelerate trials and then instal AWS. But even now, 34 years on AWS has been installed on less than two-thirds of the network.

PRESERVATION

Five Stanier Pacifics are preserved and all but one can be steamed. Following a life in public service of 31 years from 1933 to 1964, a further 24 years have elapsed from 1963 to 1986 since the five were saved. Since the first steps taken in 1961 to secure preservation both privately and nationally many changes have taken place, no one having expected two decades ago that steamed-hauled specials would again run on British Railways once steam traction had been superseded. Much has been written and many illustrations published about the restoration and running of Stanier Pacifics since 1963; thus it is sufficient in this volume to give a simple outline of events that have taken place over the last twenty years. The five preserved are Nos 6201, 6203, 6229, 6233 and 6235.

No 6201 *PRINCESS ELIZABETH*

This was the first for which a movement to ensure that it was not scrapped was undertaken, the only one of the five secured by enthusiasts' efforts! Negotiations started in the summer of 1961 and purchase by the Princess Elizabeth Preservation Society was completed during July 1963. The locomotive was moved from storage at Carlisle Upperby under its own steam by way of Leeds to Saltley where it was prepared for towing to the Dowty Railway Preservation Society's site at Ashchurch. Early work enabled steaming to take place in 1965 and continued efforts, particularly in 1973–5, gained for its owners the Association of Railway Preservation Societies' Preservation Award for 1976 in recognition of their success, especially in view of the limited equipment that had been available to the restorers. In April 1976 No 6201 was weighed at Swindon Works and in addition the axles were ultrasonically tested. Immediately afterwards the locomotive went by way of the Severn Tunnel to its new home at Hereford, Bulmers the cider makers being the host. Late in 1975 No 6201 was included in the list of those privately-owned locomotives that would be allowed to work trains on British Railways and it was 'allocated' to the West-North route between Newport, Hereford, Shrewsbury and Chester, hence its move to Hereford.

Movement away from Ashchurch had include visit to a 'Tyseley at Home' on 3 March 1971 inclusion in the Rail 150 Exhibition at Shil Works for the week before the Rail 150 Cavalc between Shildon and Heighington on 31 Aug 1975. Its display had been sponsored Darchem Limited.

Over the winter and spring of 1975–6 fi preparations were made for the first book public outing on 5 June 1976 when No 6201 to work from Hereford to Chester and back w the 'Stanier Comemmoration' special, but owners very generously allowed the locomotiv stand in for GWR 4–6–0 No 6000 *King Georg* which was found to be unfit for its spec between Hereford and Shrewsbury on 24 A 1975; this gesture by the Princess Elizab Preservation Society, despite pre-empting own plans, ensured that steam enthusiasts w not disappointed that day.

No 6201 was a participant in the Cavalcade the 150th Anniversary of the Liverpool Manchester Railway on 24 to 26 May 1980 an month later while still in the north-west between Manchester Victoria and Edge Hill 29 June 1980, going further north to vi Steamtown, Carnforth, on 25 August 1980. Sir then *Princess Elizabeth* has remained based Hereford and worked specials from there; it ha major overhaul in 1982–3.

No 6203 *PRINCESS MARGARET ROSE*

In May 1963 No 6203 arrived for installation a static exhibit at Butlin's Holiday Camp Pwllheli and remained there until it was offer 'on loan' to the Midland Railway Centre in Ap 1974. Preparations to move to Derby by rail to until May 1975, when at last it left the camp the 11th over a specially-made rail connection. Derby No 6203 was on exhibition at two wor

(*above*) Motion details of the beautifully preserved 6201 *Princess Elizabeth*, at Hereford on 20 May 19 *Roger Siviter.*

(*below*) Again on 20 May 1978 No 6201 *Princ Elizabeth* in pristine condition crosses the River near Chester race course with its return booking Hereford. *Roger Siviter.*

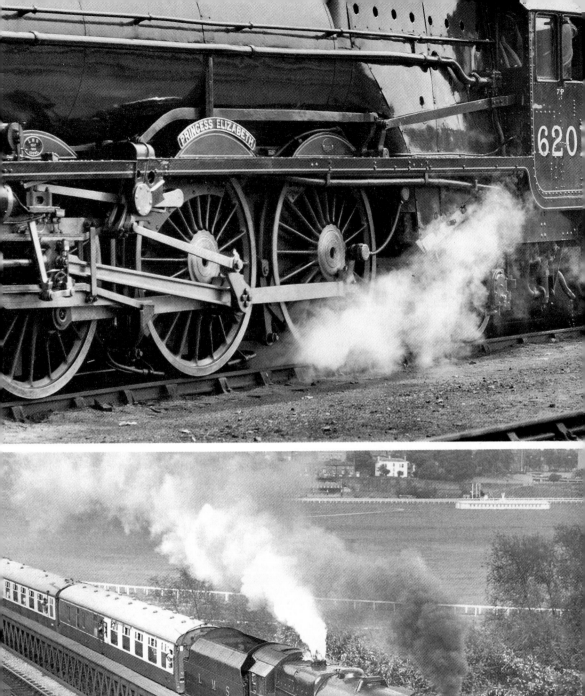

open days that summer and finally arrived at the Butterley site of the Midland Railway Trust in October 1975. Although sometimes steamed No 6203 is not on the list of locomotives that can be used on steam specials on British Railways.

No 46229 DUCHESS OF HAMILTON

Butlin's acquired No 46229 and installed it at the Minehead Holiday Camp in April 1964. It was not until 13 March 1975 that No 6229 left Minehead so that it could be housed in the National Railway Museum. Initially the locomotive was towed to Swindon for mechanical attention and repainting and then in May 1976 it was moved to York. Once in full working order *Duchess of Hamilton* achieved a substantial mileage on the Settle & Carlisle line, the first trip taking place on 10 May 1980, on the Cumbrian

Coast steam duties, based on Carnforth, York to Scarborough and Leeds steam speci In addition to appearing in the 150th Liverpoo Manchester celebrations, following *Prin Elizabeth* in the procession, No 6229 ran fr Liverpool Lime Street to Manchester Victoria 14 September 1980 and then between Li Street and York, via Standedge and Leeds on November 1980 to celebrate the 15 anniversary of carriage of post by rail. Arriva York, due to an easy timing, was 20 minutes ea at 2.48pm. The Post Office issued special cov for the occasion. Some runs have also been m on the North-to-West route between Shrewsb and Newport, initially on 31 October 1982.

As *Duchess of Hamilton* is not owned by NRM its upkeep is in the hands of the Friend the National Railway Museum. To facili steam workings it was necessary to insta turntable at Scarborough at the old motive po depot site at Seamer Road, using the origi

Smoke and steam as No 46229 *Duchess of Hamilton* passes Wennington on its way to Hellifield on 12 April 1982. *Roger Siviter*.

No 46229 *Duchess of Hamilton* makes its way south near Dent on the Settle & Carlisle line on 20 September 1984. *Roger Siviter.*

urntable pit; the turntable came from Gateshead and was lengthened and fitted with a diesel-electric drive. No 6229 was used to test the new facility.

On 16 March 1985 *Duchess of Hamilton* broke new ground by working a special from Eaglescliff to Newcastle-upon-Tyne via Durham and continuing by way of Carlisle and the Settle route to Leeds. Since then No 46229 has been engaged in working the 'Shakespeare Limited' Sunday specials from Marylebone to Stratford-on-Avon via Banbury and Leamington, the first on 12 May 1985.

No 6233 *DUCHESS OF SUTHERLAND*

The third locomotive acquired by Butlins was put on show at the Heads-of-Ayr Holiday Camp in Scotland, arriving there in October 1964, the tender on the 19th, the locomotive on the 21st. When it was decided that the holiday camp was no longer a suitable site, arrangements were made to move No 6233 to Bressingham, leaving Heads-of-Ayr on 1 March and then towed to Norfolk. It was intended to finish the journey by road from Thetford, but during transit the locomotive was made a 'Ward of Court'! This arose from an application by the Lakeside Railway Estates, Carnforth, that the transfer should have been the subject of a postal ballot of the Transport Trust, but on the day set for the hearing in Leeds, 1 March, the application was withdrawn — it all seems to have been an expensive mis-understanding. The journey from Norwich where *Duchess of Sutherland* had stood in the interval was completed by road on 21 March and now the locomotive is maintained in working order, but isolated from the tracks of British Railways.

No 46235 *CITY OF BIRMINGHAM*

Alone of the five, *City of Birmingham* is non-working, being situated in the Birmingham Museum of Science and Industry, Newhall Street, Birmingham. It was prepared by British Railways and stored at Nuneaton shed until it was moved to its permanent site in May 1966 at a cost of £1,158. The locomotive and tender were put into place first and the hall built round them!

INDEX